MEN
WHO
LOVE
Too Little

Other books that are available and can be ordered through
Fresh Start Seminars,
63 Chestnut Road, Paoli, PA 19301,
1-800-882-2799:

Fresh Start Divorce Recovery Workbook
by Bob Burns and Thomas Whiteman, Ph.D.
Fresh Start Single Parenting Workbook
by Thomas Whiteman, Ph.D., with Randy Petersen
Innocent Victims
by Thomas Whiteman, Ph.D.
Love Gone Wrong
by Thomas Whiteman, Ph.D., and Randy Petersen
Becoming Your Own Best Friend
by Thomas Whiteman, Ph.D., and Randy Petersen
Flying Solo: Devotionals for the Single Again
by Thomas Whiteman, Ph.D., and Randy Petersen
When Your Son or Daughter Is Going Through a Divorce
by Thomas Whiteman, Ph.D., and Debbie Barr

THOMAS NELSON PUBLISHERS
Nashville • Atlanta • London • Vancouver

Published in Nashville, Tennessee, by Thomas Nelson, Inc., Publishers, and distributed in Canada by Word Communications, Ltd., Richmond, British Columbia.

Library of Congress Cataloging-in-Publication Data

Whiteman, Tom.
Men who love too little / Thomas Whiteman, Randy Petersen.
p. cm.
Includes bibliographical references.
ISBN 0-8407-9173-9 (paperback)
1. Men—Psychology. 2. Sex differences (Psychology) 3. Man-woman relationships. 4. Marriage—Religious aspects—Christianity. I. Petersen, Randy. II. Title.
HQ1090.W48 1995
155.3'32—dc20 94-24637
CIP

Printed in the United States of America.

1 2 3 4 5 6 — 00 99 98 97 96 95

Contents

Preface

We have made every attempt to present the real-life situations that we have come across while preserving the privacy of the people involved. Names and some details have been changed. Some stories are composites, merging true facts from different cases.

We would like to thank Tom's colleagues at Life Counseling Services, especially Vince Gallagher, Melanie van Pletsen, and Cheryl Smith, who added input and stories for this book. We would also like to acknowledge Barbara Sandel Wirth, who went home to be with the Lord June 20, 1994. She was a trusted friend, a valuable colleague, and a wonderful counselor. Many of her clients have echoed the comment, "She was Jesus to me," because she reflected His love and healing in their lives. I can think of no greater tribute to Barb.

Tom lovingly acknowledges his wife, Lori. He can certainly be unloving at times, but without her understanding, coping, and nudging, he would surely be worse. Randy extends thanks to the Hope Church Singles Group for their support and prayers.

Introduction

"I hate men!"

The words of this woman are still ringing in my ears. She had just sat through one of my seminar sessions, and instead of hearing how she might change, she came to the conclusion that *men* were to blame. "They are all cold, insensitive jerks!"

"Does that include me?" I asked sheepishly.

She wasn't sure how to answer.

I hear similar themes from women at our seminars, particularly those who have been through a divorce, everywhere I go. But the more I look into this, the more I see that you can't divide up our whole gender like sheep and goats: "This guy's nice, this guy's a jerk, here's another jerk, oh, this one's nice." I've seen some nice qualities in men who treated their wives badly. And though I generally consider myself a nice guy, I have to admit to some jerklike qualities. And certainly a multitude of women will testify that they married nice guys who gradually *became* jerks.

Is there something in the Y chromosome that threatens to make all of us men cold, insensitive, selfish, and rude?

Well, yes. We'll talk about that a bit later.

OUT OF BALANCE

In 1985, Robin Norwood wrote the best-selling book *Women Who Love Too Much*. This book did not apply to every female, but it described the state of many women—getting into unhealthy relationships by being too giving, too nurturing, and perhaps loving too much. My cowriter, Randy Petersen, and I recently wrote about addictive relationships in *Love Gone Wrong*. As we did our research, we found the overwhelming majority of relationship addicts were women. Why are women especially susceptible to such imbalance? Some have hypothesized that women are by nature more nurturing and that this characteristic can easily go out of balance, exceeding healthy limits. When women find their personal value in being *of use* to someone else—surprise!—they get *used*. Sometimes *abused*.

This book is on the flip side of that issue. If women love too much, are men loving too little? Are men born to be users and abusers, or do they learn this behavior? We hypothesize that several basically male traits—taken to an extreme—can become very unhealthy for men and the women who love them.

THREE STEPS

This is not a drum-pounding call to get back to the grunting and grasping of the archetypal male. Nor is it a plea for men to become more like women. I believe in the utter equality of men and women—we have equal value in God's eyes, and we should be equal in each other's eyes. But equal does not mean identical. Besides the obvious physical differences, men and women are different emotionally and mentally. These differences do not make one gender better than the other. But if we are to live together profitably, we must recognize these differences and adapt to them.

So our target audience for this book is women—women who are dealing with men who love too little. Men may gain some insights into their own behavior, but we mainly want to help women cope with difficult relationships. We will offer three aspects of practical advice again and again: understand, cope, and nudge.

First, you must *understand* why your man acts as he does. Many wives assume that they are to blame for their husbands' bad behavior. This is probably not so. You need to understand some underlying reasons.

Second, you need to *cope* with the situation. If your man is too angry, too passive, or too self-centered, he will probably not change a lot. How will you deal with him?

Finally, you may *nudge* your man to change in some small ways. Don't push, and don't expect a major turnabout. But there are some ways that you might moderate some of your man's more problematic behavior.

WHERE WE'RE GOING

The first part of the book covers some general aspects of maleness. These traits apply to most men (though not all, and in different degrees). These are not in themselves negative traits, but when they go awry, you may have difficulties.

The second part focuses on seven specific types of men who love too little:

1. The angry man
2. The passive, or emotionally shutdown, man

3. The passive-aggressive man
4. The compulsive, or addicted, man
5. The controlling man
6. The self-absorbed man
7. The commitment-phobic man

You may find your husband or boyfriend in here. Even if you don't, you may want to skim these chapters to pick up some practical tips that you can transfer to your situation.

The third part gives some practical models for changing difficult relationships. Once again, you can't expect instant success, but this part should help you with activities, language, and habits that could improve your situation.

A FEW CAUTIONS

Much of this book is written in generalities. If we say, "Men tend to be this way," or "Women tend to be that way," we are not saying that every man or woman is like that. But we are talking in scientifically accepted generalities.

Please do not assume that we're saying that men are better than women. If we say that women are more verbal than men, do we mean they talk too much? No! Please avoid value judgments of these characteristics.

And we may have some blind spots. Yet we do offer the fruits of our research and what I've learned from years of counseling men, women, and couples. In addition, I've talked with thousands of divorced men and women in our Fresh Start Seminars—people who have been in the trenches of tough relationships. They have taught me much.

MEN
WHO
LOVE
Too Little

Part 1

Characteristics of Men

Chapter One

Is There a Problem Here?

"How are things at home?"

I'll ask a husband this question in a counseling session, and he'll shrug and say, "Fine, I guess."

But when I ask the same question of his wife, I'm apt to get an earful.

In a survey that appeared in *Medical Aspects of Sexuality*, four hundred leading psychiatrists were asked why marriages fail. Forty-five percent of them said that the primary cause of divorce in America was the husband's inability or unwillingness to communicate his feelings or to be emotionally vulnerable in the relationship.[1] In essence, men did not know the language of love.

Today, twenty years later, I hear similar themes from singles groups throughout the country. Single women wonder why men seem unable or unwilling to commit to a relationship. In the singles ministry in my church, I surveyed more than one hundred women to find what they would like to change in the men of their group. The vast majority of the responses fell into three basic categories.

First, they wanted men to be more open and more honest within relationships. They were tired of the macho facade, and they wished that the men could feel the freedom to be more expressive and vulnerable.

Second, they talked about the men's unwillingness to commit themselves to a relationship. They felt that the men often stayed aloof and distant, and were unwilling to express love or affection (except, of course, for sexual conquest).

Third, they described men's insensitivity or indifference toward the women's needs and interests. They felt that men seldom cared about what women thought or felt. On the whole, they said, men were not good listeners.

MISSING EACH OTHER

In the musical *My Fair Lady*, Professor Higgins asks the sexist question "Why can't a woman be more like a man?" From his point of view, that seemed to be a reasonable question. Billions of men through the ages would agree. Male behavior is direct, simple, logical. But women—who can understand them?

In a local bookstore not long ago, I saw a new book titled *What Men Understand About Women*. I picked it up and opened it. All of the pages are blank.

This nonbook exemplifies the problem. Most men don't even have a clue that there is a problem. Their partners are unsatisfied and frustrated, but these men think their relationships are fine.

We are missing each other, like two ships that pass in the night. Well, you want two ships to miss each other; otherwise they'd collide. It's like figure skater Dean throwing his partner Torvill in the air for a dramatic jump and then bending down to tie his skatelaces. She expects him to be there, she needs him to be there, but he's not. Men and women have dramatically different expectations and needs, but most of us don't realize that. How can we be missing each other so drastically?

In a survey of one thousand people, Dr. Michael McGill, author of *Changing Him, Changing Her*, found that the change women wanted most was for men to talk about their feelings. No surprise there. That corresponds with what I found in my church singles group. But the change that men wanted most was to be understood without having to talk about their feelings.[2]

BLINDED OR BELLIGERENT

Men deal with these differences in several ways. Some truly try to understand the ways of women and adapt their own behavior accordingly. But I find two negative approaches to the differences: Some men are blinded, and others are belligerent.

The blinded man usually doesn't have a clue that he's doing anything wrong. Or if you manage to convince him something's wrong, he has no idea what it is. He is not aware that he loves too little. He feels a certain love for his woman, and he expresses it in what he considers appropriate ways. Yet the message doesn't come through. He is completely missing the needs of the woman he claims to love.

Many men blithely live their lives their own way, assuming that their wives are along for the ride.

The blinded man means well but doesn't know any better. He needs to be informed of your needs. You need to communicate how you're feeling and thinking. This isn't always easy, but the communication should yield a rich give-and-take relationship.

The belligerent man may be aware of his differences with the woman in his life, but he doesn't care. "Let her adjust to me" is his attitude. In many cases, such men come from homes that revolved around their fathers. In their minds, the man is the king of his castle and will bend to no one.

Belligerent men often need to be in control and can be overly self-centered or just angry. If you don't feel loved by such a man, tough. "Get used to it," he declares.

If you are married to a belligerent man, the prognosis is not good. But it's not hopeless. You may be able to understand some of the behavior that presently bothers you and even accept it. You may learn to live with the differences between you and your man. And you may even nudge your partner in the right direction. As you appreciate and support his distinctively male qualities, you may find a way to soften his excesses.

Male-Female Wish List[3]

Men wish women would	*Women wish men would*
Talk less	Talk more
Demand less help	Be more willing to help
Show more emotional stability	Express more emotion
Be more physical	Be more romantic/less physical
Be more logical	Be more spontaneous
Be less concerned about their looks	Be more considerate of their feelings
Like sports more	Pay more attention to their interests
Hurry up getting ready	Be more patient

A UNIQUE POINT IN HISTORY

Male roles have changed dramatically in Western culture over the past several decades. This has created a gender gap and an expectation gap between men and women, which is why we "miss" each other so much.

This century has seen tremendous changes in the roles of men and women. The social revolution of the 1960s and the economic need of the 1970s spawned a full-fledged feminist movement that challenged the millennia-old tradition of male dominance.

Equality became the buzzword. Women were proving themselves to be just as skilled, just as intelligent, just as important as men. But for a while, "equal to" was taken to mean "the same as."

It was a confusing time. Men were urged to take sensitivity training and get in touch with their feelings. Women were urged to take assertiveness training and look out for number one.

For a while, it was refreshing for some people. Men were free to let down the macho image and explore their feminine side. But a new image was being forged, and it had the feeling of clothing that didn't quite fit. Both men and women squirmed with uneasiness under the new assumptions.

Bob Hicks put it this way in his book *Uneasy Manhood*:

> Many women want men to be more feminine, but if they will admit it, they still want men to be strong. That's quite a bind for men! Women want men to be strong when they need strength, but they want sensitive caring males when they need those qualities. And of course, men have to guess which women want or need at any given moment.[4]

After a decade or two of male bashing, many men have decided that it's okay to be men. And shocking new evidence indicates that men and women are actually different—biologically different, and beyond just body parts. Our chemistry is different. Our brains are different. All of that creates different strengths and weaknesses and, well, *differences*.[5]

FREE TO BE MEN

The social revolution of the 1960s and 1970s set us free from the narrow role models of past generations—the tough, resilient heroes; the men who were cool under pressure, not showing emotion. We are free to be who we are, *men*. Men who laugh and love and sulk and thunder. Men who can celebrate our male distinctives and not feel guilty when women don't find us feminine enough. But also men who are secure enough to cry, to listen, to open up a little about our needs. We are free to be real people, real men.

Consider the Differences[6]

Male	***Female***
Thicker skulls	Lighter bones
Joints tighter	More flexibility
More muscle	More fat
Thicker skin	Wrinkle earlier
Greater risk of reading disabilities	More verbal
More die within 3 months of birth	Live longer
Brain more compartmentalized	More connectors between two hemispheres
Drawn to objects, sports	More relational
More mechanical abilities	More emotional
More aggressive and competitive	More process oriented and holistic
Store fat above the waist	Store fat on hips and thighs
More easily aroused	Better sense of smell

But does that mean we have to go back to the battle of the sexes? Are we destined for this stalemate in which neither side understands the other and no one speaks the same language?

No. I believe that God has made both men and women to be very different, and yet to complement and challenge one another. Instead of throwing our hands up in disgust and bewilderment, we should seek to understand our differences and honor them.

Chapter Two

Are Men's Brains Different?

Men's brains are different from women's. In the second month of pregnancy, the male brain is flooded with testosterone, which radically alters its composition. This event begins a series of complex changes in the brain that will cause the male to look, act, and think differently.[1]

The human brain is divided into two sections, the right hemisphere and the left hemisphere. Each side is responsible for different functions.

In the female brain, there are more connecting fibers and the fibers are larger than in the male brain. This means that females have a greater tendency to use both sides of the brain simultaneously. They are more verbal and relational, but they also tend to use more emotion when processing information and when communicating.

Men, on the other hand, tend to use the left side of the brain more and therefore use more logic and rational thought.

Exceptions to this left-brain preference can be found in musicians, artists, and generally more creative males.

Men also tend to have better eye-hand coordination (which helps them in many sports) and better spatial skills (which helps with mechanical abilities, map reading, etc.). From birth, males are drawn more to objects and females to faces and people.

The Two Hemispheres

This general list of commonly accepted brain functions has been adapted from a list in *Male and Female Realities* by Joe Tannenbaum.[2] Many men are left-brain dominant, while women tend to use both sides simultaneously. Artistic, creative, and musical people of both sexes are usually right-brain dominant.

Left Brain	***Right Brain***
Verbal—using words to name, describe, and define	Nonverbal—awareness of objects
Analytic—figuring things out logically, step by step	Synthetic—putting ideas together to form concepts
Sequential—keeping track of time, order, and consequences	Holistic—having less sense of time, more sense of whole picture, overall pattern
Rational—determining positions by facts and reasoning	Emotional—thinking based in feelings
Logical and linear—reaching conclusions based on logic, one thought following another	Intuitive—understanding situations based on emotion, hunches, or visual images

---

More significantly, men are better able to separate their emotions from their intellect due to the smaller and fewer connecting fibers between the two sides of the brain. This ability to compartmentalize their thinking has dramatic implications for men and women in relationships. This aspect of men's thinking leads us to the first male characteristic we'll consider in our search for why men seem to love too little.

But before I go into greater detail, I need to reiterate that in all of these characteristics, I am speaking of men in general. Most men will have these traits to some degree, but so will some women.

CHARACTERISTIC #1: MEN HAVE THE ABILITY TO COMPARTMENTALIZE THEIR THINKING

- After a long, intense relationship, Joe and Ginger decide to call it quits. It's a mutual thing—they both realize they're not right for each other. Still, Ginger sinks into a depression, while Joe meets another woman a few days later and asks her out, with no apparent regrets regarding Ginger.
- Sam has a shouting match with his wife, Sheila, on a Sunday morning. They continue the argument in the car on the way to church. But once inside the church door, Sam is smiling, shaking hands with people in the lobby, while Sheila is in a foul mood for the rest of the day.
- Dave comes home from work brooding. He rejects Jan's attempts to console him. He is silent at dinner and parks himself in front of the TV all night, resisting any conversation with his wife. But at bedtime he becomes suddenly amorous, trying to ignite instant romance.

In each case, the man closes one door and opens another. He shuts off one type of thinking and begins a new one. The woman has a hard time following that pattern. For her, the doors stay open. Emotion and logic and romance and communication all bleed together.

This characteristic of men—the ability to compartmentalize—can be a tremendous strength, but it is a source of considerable misunderstanding between men and women. Men can seem cold, callous, and unemotional because they have the ability to turn off their emotions. On the other hand, men often consider women overemotional and irrational merely because emotion and logic interact more in women's minds.

Choosing to Think Differently

In my work as a therapist, I discovered that my male assumptions were sabotaging my work with some female clients. Frequently, while counseling women who were depressed or lacked self-confidence, I would say, "Just think about all of the things you should be happy about," or "Think about those less fortunate than yourself." This reframing of life's circumstances usually improves my moods within a matter of hours. I was able to change my moods (right brain) by intellectually focusing on what I knew was true (left brain). I literally set aside how I was feeling and chose to think and feel differently.

This approach worked for me, as I said, but it wasn't working with most of my female clients.

The women found it difficult to compartmentalize their thinking. They were using both sides of the brain at once, and they were hard-pressed to focus on the rational while ignoring their emotions.

I suspect that thousands of couples have experienced this in their conversations, though they may not have figured it out yet. The problem is that she can't close the emotional door and open the rational. Both are open all the time. She needs emotional stimuli as well as rational argument to overcome her negative feelings. An accepting hug might mean more than a logical statement in a case like this.

There's a case of a man assuming that a woman thinks in a male way. But often a woman assumes that a man thinks in a female way. She finds it hard to understand how a man turns off his feelings regarding something (or someone) that's important to him. Have you ever had this conversation?

SHE: Did you think about me today, dear?

HE: Uuuhhhh. Let me think. Did I think about you? Let's see. What happened today?

SHE: You didn't, did you? I must not mean anything to you!

HE: But you do! I'm sure I thought of you. I'm just trying to remember . . .

The truth is, he probably didn't unless something specific came up. At work, men tend to think about work. When they come home, they may try to shut out work and focus on their families. A woman may be perplexed by how a man can *not* think about the most important person in his life for eight hours or so. But it's that compartmentalizing ability. Close that door; open this one. She'll still be there when you open that door again.

This ability can be an advantage when it comes to managing our emotions, but it can also enable us to stuff certain emotions in an unhealthy way. We have the ability to shut one door and open another, to turn off anger to focus on something else. But when we open that door again, the anger is still there, and it may gnaw away at us while we're not paying attention. Compartmentalizing may keep a man from dealing with his true feelings because he can so easily shut them away.

Irresponsible compartmentalizing can also sear a man's conscience, as guilt feelings are shut away. Violent crimes, cutthroat business decisions, and abusive relationships are all examples of how the ability to shut off emotions can be misused.

Seconding the Emotion

Women often think of men as being unemotional. Men often think of women as being overemotional. Both misunderstandings stem from this compartmentalizing quality. With all the connecting brain fibers, both sides of the brain tend to be involved in everything women do. Emotion and logic flow together. It's not that women are irrational; they're just not exclusively rational.

But men are not necessarily unemotional, either. They're just not controlled by emotion. When it gets to a bothersome level, they can shut the door. It's true that boys are usually not taught to express their emotions, but I don't think that's the whole story. I think boys learn early that emotions can get in the way. When you're crying, it's hard to talk or breathe or see. Emotions can keep you from accomplishing what you want to accomplish; therefore, they must be closely regulated. And males, without as many connecting brain fibers, have the ability to guard their emotions. It doesn't mean the emotions aren't there. They're just locked in their room.

Chapter Three

Look Who's Talking!

Tim Allen is on to something. Frequently on the hit TV comedy "Home Improvement," his character makes noises. He grunts and growls and mumbles and moans. The inflection of his voice makes it clear how he's feeling, though you can't quite put it into words. And that's exactly the point. Men don't put things into words.

Man's ability to compartmentalize is not the only characteristic that has been attributed to the brain differences between the sexes. There are actually hundreds of subtle differences that are beyond the scope of this book. Yet one very obvious difference is in the ability to verbalize feelings.

CHARACTERISTIC #2: MEN ARE LESS VERBAL THAN WOMEN

I've been told that on average, men speak about ten thousand words per day. Women, on the other hand, speak about twenty-five thousand words a day. Don't ask me who counted. But this estimate seems accurate in light of the research on the verbal skills of both men and women.

The man stops talking long before the woman does. The women tend to think their husbands are unusually quiet (and they often fear their husbands are losing interest in them). The men tend to think their wives are unusually talkative.

But these verbal differences can cause serious trouble in a relationship if the partners take it personally. The simple truth is that women, on average, talk more than men do because their brains allow them to talk more freely. When both partners understand these basic tendencies, they can make allowances for each other's behavior.

Baby Talk

The verbal differences between males and females are apparent very early. By age two, the language skills of girls are developing more quickly than those of boys. By age four, the differences are pronounced. Girls speak at a younger age, have better enunciation, and are generally better readers. (Three-quarters of reading disabilities are found in boys.) Girls are also better at grasping verbal concepts, making analogies, and comprehending language.[1]

Losing Situations

Perhaps you were in a discussion with your husband or boyfriend that suddenly became an argument, but you're not sure how. Somehow you touched a nerve, you threatened his authority, and he became defensive. Suddenly, the exchange of opinions or information became a matter of winning and losing. And the more you tried to clarify the matter, using your verbal skills, the more frustrated he became.

Most men are not verbally impaired. Men can talk. Men

can express their feelings. They just can't do it as well as women can. But because they find themselves at a disadvantage, they choose not to get into verbal situations.

What happens in the discussion-turned-argument is that the man finds himself losing.

In such cases, feeling verbally overwhelmed, some men play dirty. They may resort to physical abuse, exercising power in an area where they have the advantage. More often, men will practice verbal abuse to try to gain control of the situation.

Even more often, men will withdraw from verbal interaction. "If I can't win at this game, then I'd rather not play." They'll nod and grunt. They'll leave the room. They'll avoid their wives. Withdrawal can happen in big ways or small ways.

John Gray writes about the "cave" that men enter when they have a problem to solve or when they want to recover from stress. He's speaking of this tendency to withdraw. By contrast, in similar situations, women tend to talk it out. These are radically different problem-solving strategies.

"When a man is stuck in his cave," Gray writes, "he is powerless to give his partner the quality attention she deserves." Gray notes that a man can "listen" with 5 percent of his mind—and he can probably maintain the appropriate nodding and grunting—but the other 95 percent is in the "cave," mulling over some issue or escaping from it all. "If he were to come home and talk about all his problems," Gray adds, "then she could be more compassionate. Instead . . . she feels he is ignoring her. She can tell he is upset but mistakenly assumes he doesn't care about her because he isn't talking to her."[2]

Getting in Touch

But the mere fact that men are less verbal is only part of the problem, right? You could deal with that. But when men do talk, it's always about machines or numbers or maybe, if you're lucky, ideas. Why can't they talk about how they feel?

Guys feel uncomfortable talking about their feelings. And they feel very uncomfortable listening to other guys sharing their feelings.

This characteristic is probably a combination of brain and hormonal differences along with cultural pressures on men. For example, if a particular man is born with more verbal abilities and is more in touch with his emotions, he probably learns at a very young age that it is not appropriate to talk with other guys about certain things.

Therefore, even when men are emotional and perhaps feel that they need to talk, they have probably been trained to keep quiet. Why? To do otherwise, they fear, would appear feminine, weak, or silly. Most men want to avoid these labels at all costs.

Men have many layers of training placed on us by parents (especially fathers), peers, society, the media, besides our genetic predisposition. The layers have built up since the time we were born and continue to build up. Subtle messages—"Men don't cry" or "Don't be a sissy"—seem small at the time but can have lifelong effects. We shield ourselves by these layers of repression and control. We don't talk, don't feel, and don't trust. Then we get married, and our wives say, "Open up. Talk to me. Trust me."

It's not as easy as it might seem.

Chapter Four

Let's Get Together

One of the most ancient of stories, from the Greek bard Homer, is the *Odyssey*, the story of Odysseus. The image that comes to my mind now is one of the events from his trip home. Odysseus's ship is blown off course. The rocky shore they must sail by is inhabited by beautiful women who sing to the sailors, only to lead them to their deaths. Odysseus's crew survive by filling their ears with wax and tying themselves to the mast. They are able to sail through safely, ignoring the song of the women on the shore.

The story is probably supposed to symbolize the resisting of temptation, but I just see a boatload of men ignoring the voices of women. If they listen, they will only crash and drown. In other words, stick with the guys; women will ruin your life.

I'm sure many women have felt that their husbands had wax in their ears. And it's not just a matter of entering into conversations. It's that he doesn't seem interested in developing his relationship with you. That can be agonizing when so much of your life revolves around your man, yet he sits there unmoved—as if he couldn't care less. Is that just the way men are?

Unfortunately, yes. To a degree.

CHARACTERISTIC #3: MEN ARE LESS RELATIONAL THAN WOMEN

Odysseus has had many successors as the lonesome hero in literature through the centuries. Now movies have carried on the tradition. The male hero is on a quest—for success, for peace of mind, for justice—and no one quite understands him. Women may be crazy about him, but even they don't understand him. He loves them and leaves them and stalks off toward his next adventure. Maybe he has a buddy that he bonds with, like Butch Cassidy and the Sundance Kid. But even that friendship is shared in shorthand. They never talk much about their feelings. They just join forces and look out for each other.

For these heroes, relationships would get in the way.

Men tend to have difficulty building deep relationships. Women, on the other hand, seem especially relationship oriented.

Reasons for Relationships

So is there a biological predisposition in women toward relationships with other people? Many scholars are suggesting that. As we have already seen, the connecting fibers between the hemispheres of the brain enable women to talk more freely about their emotions, which helps them deepen relationships. Men, who guard their emotions more, tend to keep their relationships on surface levels.

But this difference between the sexes is culturally conditioned as well. Men learn not to express their emotions, especially around other men.

Men *can* show emotion with each other in certain arenas. Football teammates dance, hug, slap fannies, and jump for joy on national television. War buddies or police partners become as close as any two humans can get when they are exposed to danger or death. Many carry a common bond that crosses all time and distance.

Perhaps men can grow close only in parallel relationships. That is, if two or more men are working toward a common goal, they are moving in parallel lines toward that goal. Side by side, a relationship can develop.

Where do these relational rules for men come from? I believe they are largely cultural. There are many cultures in which men hug, kiss, or hold hands in public. But in American culture, we learn at a very young age that these things are not acceptable.

Male-Female Relationships

What about our relationships with women? Well, once again we need to own up to our generalities. Men are not incapable of establishing good relationships. For many men, relationships aren't a high priority; relationships occur on the way to something else. We saw that in the parallel nature of male-male friendships. It's also true of many male-female relationships.

My friend Richard told me that some of his best friendships are with women he wanted to date. He proudly described the strategy he has used for more than a decade. "Sometimes I'll really like a girl who's not that interested in me," he said. "So I'll say, 'No problem. Let's just be friends.' And I mean that. I want to get to know her. So we go out to dinner as friends. Or we go to a movie as friends. And the whole time we're getting to know each other with no pressure, no worries."

Most of those friendships, Richard said, have lasted; some have even withstood romantic breakups. I'm still not sure he's being entirely honest. Still, it illustrates my point that men often establish relationships on the way to something else. With women, that something else is often romance.

I don't mean to imply that all male-female friendships are romantic or quasi-romantic. In fact, I have often thought that some of the best friendships a man can have are with women he is not romantically involved with. In a male-male friendship, both parties put up walls that interfere with forming a solid relationship. In a male-female friendship, there's only one wall (his). And when romance is not involved, it keeps him honest. He won't be using the tools of relationship building for a different purpose.

That's exactly what happens in many marriages. A man may strive to win a woman without any true relationship building. It's a quest, like Odysseus's trip home, but it's very different from day-to-day life. On this quest, a man learns to use the woman's tools of relationship building: cards, flowers, little gifts, walks, talks, vulnerability. Some of them may seem silly to the man, but he'll use them because he's on a quest. They are the most effective ways to win her heart.

I don't want to be too cynical here. Some men are truly interested in building deep relationships with the women they court, but there is usually (at least in some degree) this matter of achievement. If I want to win this woman, I'll do whatever it takes. And that may mean that I present a false image of my relational ability.

More than a few women have been shocked to find, after the marriage, that their husbands weren't the loving men they pretended to be. When the quest was over, when the prize was won, the men turned into giant slugs.

Men will regularly do the work of marriage, showing their loyalty by being a good husband—bringing home a paycheck, doing chores, maybe even buying gifts. But women are usually looking for something much different: "I don't want things. I want you! I want us to talk, relate, and share our whole selves with each other."

Is There Hope for Us?

Is there any hope for those of us who are relationally impaired? I think so. Some men are blinded to their weaknesses. With considerable effort and some careful compromises, they should be able to overcome their relational deficiencies and establish satisfying relationships with their partners—though there will always be some differences. Yet other men are belligerent about their privacy, insisting that women should just get used to them because they are not about to change.

Since women are asking us to open up, to talk, and to relate to them better, what is holding us back? We've already identified our impairments, but we can't stop there. We may not be as verbal or relational, but when we have a goal and are willing to work, we can be good at resolving our problems. But it takes years of work and lots of patience—from our women and ourselves.

Chapter Five

Me Hunter Man!

The brain is not the only reason for the dynamic differences between men and women. In fact, even more differences can be pinned to the hormone testosterone. That hormone triggers a chain of events creating the changes in the male brain. Testosterone is also the major suspect for many of the motivations and drives of the male.

Research indicates that both men and women have levels of testosterone in their systems, just as both have some level of female hormones. Of critical importance are the amounts. Studies have indicated that the higher the level of testosterone, the more the person demonstrates typically male traits such as body hair, lower voice, and aggressiveness. Female hormones inhibit or counteract the effects of male hormones. Therefore, males with higher testosterone levels and lower estrogen levels tend to be more aggressive and competitive, have deeper and more forceful voices, have coarser hair, and have a more active sex life.

Testosterone levels in men are highest in their teenage years, and then they decline significantly in older men. There may actually be hormonal reasons for what we think of as the mellowing of older men.

On the other hand, women's testosterone levels increase as they age. And for most, the offsetting estrogen levels decrease. As a result, women may grow facial hair, experience deepened voices, and pick up other typically male characteristics. This irony may be of some encouragement to some couples who seem hopelessly different.

CHARACTERISTIC #4: MEN TEND TO BE AGGRESSIVE AND COMPETITIVE

Anyone who knows men knows about their aggressive and competitive nature. These traits are not necessarily bad, but when they are out of balance, they become a major factor in a man's seeming to love too little. Our aggressiveness and competitiveness have led to major inventions, business deals, and a successful lifestyle for many. But they have also led to wars, violence, and unguarded greed.

I want to discuss the more subtle ways in which men are more aggressive or competitive—in our conversations and our relationships.

Quipping One Another

In her book *You Just Don't Understand,* Deborah Tannen discusses the conversational differences between men and women. She says that men tend to view other men as adversaries. We compare salaries, what our children have done, and the amount of hair we still have. It can all be very friendly. But when we do this with women, they just don't understand. Most women do not have the same competitive instinct.

With other men, we have learned how to gibe or "bust on" each other. The more we like other guys, the more we are liable to bust on them. I have my fishing buddies, and we can really give it to each other. Anything will do: the fish, the way you drive, the boots you're wearing, whatever comes to mind.

We're just playing, or so we like to think. But something deeper is going on. It's a testing, a toughening, an induction into the brotherhood of guys who can both dish it out and take it.

Even in adult life, men's conversations can be a reflection of the competitive nature. We fire quips and try to one-up each other. Who can come up with the wittiest comeback line? Deborah Tannen puts it this way:

> Men engage the world as an individual in a hierarchical, social order, in which he was either one up, or one down. In this world, conversations are negotiations in which people try to achieve and maintain the upper hand, and protect themselves from other people's attempts to put them down, and push them around. Life is a contest; a struggle to preserve independence and avoid failure.[1]

Tannen goes on to say that women's conversations are negotiations for closeness, in which people try to give confirmation and support and try to reach consensus. They find meaning and purpose in relationship to others. Inclusiveness is desired.

Boys and Men at Play and Work

These conversational patterns and styles of relating are deeply rooted in our nature and our early childhood. From our earliest friendships, we demonstrated our differences from the opposite sex. Research on boys and girls at play has found what many of us have known instinctively. Boys play in groups where there are leaders, rules, winners and losers. There is usually a clear hierarchy with the strongest and most skilled at the top. They then organize into games where skill is tested and someone comes out on top, such as ball games and races.

Girls, on the other hand, tend to group into pairs. When they play together, each one takes a turn, and they value having equal authority. Many of their games have no winners or losers, such as jumping rope, having tea parties, and playing house.

It has been fashionable lately to attribute all these differences to conditioning. For some time, the thinking was that the only reason girls play with dollhouses and boys with toy trucks is that we give dollhouses to girls and toy trucks to boys. I would agree that there is a great deal of conditioning in many families and in society at large. Men are conditioned, to some degree, to be more competitive. But research has been showing us that conditioning isn't the whole story. Even when we try to change early childhood training, we find that boys and girls are very different in the way they play.

I've observed similar dynamics in adult interactions. Men compete and challenge one another, while women tend to prefer cooperation and relationship-building tasks. Men who work together tend to form a hierarchical structure in which there is constant tension to move up the ladder. Coworkers constantly compete. Yet most of it is friendly. We enjoy the challenge to be the best at bringing in more business, increasing sales, or filling a quota. We actually push one another to do more and to be better.

At work, men value freedom, a sense of control, independence, and challenges. Women value a good challenge as well, but they also tend to look for closeness, equality, and shared experiences.

I should say that in talking about gender differences in the business world, there are almost more exceptions than rules. Like it or not, we are still in a transition phase regarding women in business. The business world tends to play by men's rules. And that means that the women who climb the ladder in business tend to be more aggressive than other women. (Note that the ladder itself is a hierarchical approach, which is more in keeping with a male outlook.)

The Warrior

Confused expectations can be a major problem for couples. Many women want their men to be aggressive enough to go gunning for that promotion at work but not so aggressive that they yell a lot around the house. Both behaviors come from the same pool of testosterone. Men often feel torn between the need to compete in a dog-eat-dog world on behalf of their families and the need to curb their aggressive impulses when dealing with their families.

In *The Masculine Journey*, Robert Hicks writes of the "warrior," an essential stage of the male life:

> It is the warrior in men that energizes them to keep going, to press toward goals, to stand their ground, to defend their personal and corporate values, even to the point of risking self. As men we war in business, in sports, in marriages, in our conversations, and with our political agendas.[2]

This is probably the major image that the modern men's movement is fighting for. Somehow, our society has villainized the warrior. It's not cool to fight anymore. Yet leaders of the men's movement see this as being an essential aspect of being men. If we can't be warriors, who are we?

Patrick Arnold calls the warrior image "one of the most important archetypes in masculine spirituality and a central male role in virtually every society since Paleolithic times," adding that it "has come to epitomize the noblest qualities of masculinity: bravery, self-sacrifice, stamina, and heroic detachment." Yet he warns that the image is under attack: "In some intellectual circles the type is viewed solely as dangerous and destructive to males."[3] And Robert Bly laments, "The fading of the warrior contributes to the collapse of civilized society."[4]

I believe that men (and the women who love them) need to acknowledge their warrior spirit and understand it. And I think they need to redeem it, harnessing its energy for positive uses.

Keeping Score

In the delightful little film *Gregory's Girl*, a teenage girl asks, "Why are boys obsessed with numbers?" She's got a point.

We talk batting averages and horsepower and cubic inches and acreage and interest rates.

What is this fascination with counting? Where does it come from? What does it mean?

It may go back to differences in the brains of males and females. Perhaps the fewer connections between hemispheres allow the logical left brain to dominate in most men. That's where the definable quantities live, on the left.

You might say that this difference governs our whole lives. A man and a woman walk into a party. She "reads" the situation. He "scores" it.

Oh, she says, that woman doesn't look happy; I wonder what's wrong.

Mmm, he says, that woman's a ten.

Ah, she says, that guy's kind of cute.

Yeah, he says, I think I could beat him one on one in basketball.

The competitive streak in men keeps them in the comparing game. And their penchant for numbers gives them the shelves on which to put their wares.

The problem is that men keep score in relationships with women. Women keep score, too, but their scoring rules are totally different. As John Gray points out, men assume that big gifts are worth a lot more than little gifts (whether these are gifts of material things, efforts, or common niceties).[5] Taking out the trash might be worth one point, but buying a diamond necklace for your wife would be worth fifty. But women tend to award one point for every gift, big or small. It's just nice to be thought of.

Men, however, are usually aware of the score (and many of us tilt it in our favor). We know how much we have done for our women and how much they owe us. If our women do favors for us, we quickly measure out how much we need to do to even the score.

We seldom talk about the scoring, though. It comes up only when there's a problem. So a man may assume that it's 55 to 18 in his favor (after all, he gave her that necklace) while the woman feels vaguely that the score must be quite a bit in her favor. Both sides feel they are owed something, and resentment builds on both sides.

Communication is crucial *before* a misunderstanding reaches a crisis point. Couples need to compare notes regularly to see what the score is, especially in view of the fact that men and women keep score so differently.

Chapter Six

Just Do It!

Imagine one man calling a male friend and saying, "Why don't you come over tonight and we'll have a cup of coffee?"

"Sure, what's up?"

"Nothing's up. I just thought we could talk."

"Talk about what? Did I do something wrong?"

"No, not at all. I just thought we could spend some time getting to know each other a little better."

"Oh, well, I'm going to be watching the ball game tonight. You're welcome to come over and watch the game with me."

It sounds strange, doesn't it? Guys don't come over to "get to know each other a little better." Yet for women, this is commonplace. For women, relationships are valuable in and of themselves. You don't need an agenda; you just get together and talk. It's enough to be together.

But men get together to do something. Men might set a goal of building the relationship, but even that is rare. Social interactions are like games—men need goals and direction.

It's not good enough to play house; we want something we can win. We have to accomplish something.

CHARACTERISTIC #5: MEN ARE GOAL-ORIENTED DOERS

We converse to exchange information and opinions. Rarely do we share feelings. If relationship building is the goal, we are usually earning respect or evaluating whether to give respect to another. There must be a purpose to our interactions—even if the purpose is no more than a game itself.

I've scheduled retreats for both women and men. Women's comments are usually along the lines of wanting more time for interaction and processing information. Men usually make comments about wanting more activities or free time in which they could do what they want (independence and control again).

This yen for accomplishment also affects the jobs we choose. Men gravitate toward positions in which they can monitor the bottom line. What have I done today? Did I win? Did I lose?

Men are what they do. This is why workaholics are mostly men. This is also why unemployment hits men so hard. A woman losing her job may panic about her financial security, but a laid-off man has sustained a blow to his identity. He feels worthless because no one wants what he does. I'm not denying that unemployed women feel bad, but action orientation makes unemployment even worse for men. Their work is at the core of their selfhood.

But action orientation spreads beyond what men do for a living. It also includes what they do on the ball field or at the workbench or in their hobby corner.

It's not just the male ego we're dealing with here (though

we will talk about that later). It's the fact that men are doers, and they define themselves by what they do.

Romancing a Woman

Goal orientation appears prominently in the male desire to win women. Our literature is full of this sort of thing. The gallant knight slays the dragon to win the fair princess as his bride. A man learns to do whatever he has to do to win a woman's heart. On a quest for love, there's no telling what a man will do.

At first blush, a woman may think it flattering to be a prize for a devoted knight. But once the conquest is gained, watch out. Without a challenge, many men become bored and disinterested, and they start looking for new challenges.

When the need for the challenge of conquest is so great, the satisfaction of found love is diminished. The grass always grows greener in that other woman's yard. Many of these single men seem to want no part of long-term commitments. The situation can be more devastating, though, when a man with this pattern gets married. He may be thrilled for a while with his new wife, but in time his eyes and mind begin to wander toward new challenges and new thrills.

In an essay on men, John Updike notes, "The sense of the chase lives in him as the key to life."[1] This male desire for accomplishment may affect even the relationships of faithfully married couples. We often see this in physical interactions. Women tend to enjoy hugs, cuddles, and kisses for their own sake. For men, they are usually a means to an end. If cuddling doesn't lead to sex, why bother?

Let's Just Get There!

Our goal orientation affects not only our relationships but also the way we approach life in general. In essence, we don't stop to smell the roses.

The father starts off the family vacation by saying, "Okay, everyone go to the bathroom before you get in the car because once we're on the road we're not stopping." Who cares about having a good time? Let's just *get there*. The whole family may be cranky, but Dad will boast that he made it to the shore in record time.

Our goal orientation can also cause men to be bored and impatient about women's interests. If a woman wants to talk about the beautiful scenery, her latest shopping trip, or a meaningful conversation with a friend, we yawn, "Is this conversation going anywhere? Is there a point to this?" Merely chatting is difficult for us because nothing gets done.

Finding Balance

Obviously, we can have fun describing these differences between men and women. But they can cause significant rifts in relationships if we fail to understand and allow for these distinctions. Problems occur when we expect our partners to be like us. When women think men are abnormal for being so goal oriented, or when men think women are abnormal for being less goal oriented, they develop false expectations. Blame enters the relationship and erodes it.

As with each distinction in this book, you need to understand your partner's level of goal orientation and learn to live with it. Perhaps you can find some creative compromises that will enable you to pool your strengths with those of your partner.

Chapter Seven

We Did It My Way

"Uh, honey, do you know where we're going?"

"Sort of."

"What do you mean 'sort of'?"

"I've been there before."

"When?"

"Last year sometime."

"But they moved."

"I know."

"So you know where we're going."

"Sort of."

"You didn't call for directions?"

"I can find it. It's not a problem."

Have you ever been on a car ride like that? He insists he knows the way, while you watch him get more and more hopelessly lost.

As you probably know from experience, this is not merely a matter of finding your way. It's a guy thing. It becomes an issue of male identity. It's bigger than both of you.

This simple example, replayed by thousands of couples in thousands of cars, touches a deep insecurity in men. Maybe it's our supposed spatial ability that makes us rise to the challenge of navigation. And certainly the woman's need for security enters in—what if you run out of gas in the middle of Saskatchewan? Female fear and male pride can escalate a spat to a world war.

But we see a similar syndrome in a man's reluctance to get help on taxes, call a repair person, or see a doctor. Why won't a man stop and ask for help? It's an issue of control.

I know where I stand. I can do it myself. Everything's under control.

CHARACTERISTIC #6: MEN LIKE TO BE IN CONTROL

"I am a rock," sang Simon and Garfunkel in the 1960s. They could have been talking about most men. A rock is strong, unmovable. And many men strive to be strong and independent, unmoved in the face of crisis or tragedy. They learn to control their emotions.

Men's desire for control starts within ourselves and fans outward to others. From childhood, males learn that it is manly to hold back tears and girlish to cry.

When we do feel, we must block out the feelings or control our response enough to demonstrate a rational reaction. As a result, we are incredibly bound up with repressed emotion, unresolved anger, and an inability to express how we feel. I believe most of us are truly blind to this. We have gotten so good at controlling our emotions that we may not even know what we feel anymore. When asked how we feel about a Super Bowl loss, we can express our frustration with our team and replay how the game could have been won. But when asked how we feel about our marriages, we say, "I feel fine. Why? What's wrong?"

Roots of Control

There may be some biological root of the male desire for self-control—those connecting fibers in the brain again—but this is certainly shaped and reinforced by our culture. Manly men don't get emotional. Warren T. Farrell says, "Boys see models of men who display material success, detachment or coolness, physical and psychological strength, leadership and apparent invulnerability. . . . Boys learn to admire and aspire to be like the role models."

Farrell lists the "Ten Commandments of Masculinity," as our culture has defined them. Here are the first two:

> 1. Thou shalt not cry or in other ways display fear, weakness, sympathy, empathy, or involvement before thy neighbor.
> 2. Thou shalt not be vulnerable but shalt honor and respect the "logical," "practical," or "intellectual"—as thou definest them.[1]

One generation of fathers passes the ideal of emotional control to the next. If we don't learn this control from parents (in word or example), we learn it from friends or perhaps from the culture at large. Boys quickly learn that it is socially unacceptable to be too emotional about things. That's what girls do—and it's important that boys distinguish themselves from girls. No one wants to be a sissy. Much of the socialization process for boys, from grade school through high school and even college, is a toughening of character, the crafting of personal shields, the development of emotional control.

Various movie stars have modeled masculinity for us in this century. By and large, the most popular actors have projected unemotional images. From John Wayne to Bogie to Clint to Arnold, we don't see many tears or fears. We see straight faces, nerves of steel, eyes that penetrate every crisis. It's interesting that Schwarzenegger's most popular role, in the Terminator films, is not that of a man at all but a machine. Androids aren't built for deep feeling.

When men do admit to crying, they often use an interesting term: "I lost it." What have they lost? Control. For men, emotional expression is not seen as a valuable commodity; it's a loss. It doesn't get you anywhere. It doesn't help anything.

That's a skewed view, an undervaluing of emotion. Yet it is deeply rooted in the male psyche. We expend a lot of energy controlling ourselves. Most of us know the toll that takes on our bodies. Men have higher rates of ulcers, heart problems, and other stress-related illnesses. Could this be because we keep such a tight grip on our bodies' natural release valves? Yet this is a way of life that men grow up with. It will not be easy to change.

Control of Others

I know a man who always has to have his way. He bullies others, bosses his kids around, and is especially overbearing to his wife. Over the years he has lost all of his friends. They come around at first because he knows how to throw his money at them. He can manipulate them with promises. But after a while, most conclude that he is not worth the trouble.

All of his children were forced to follow his wishes. From hobbies and friends to the choice of a college, Dad controlled it all—until they were old enough to get out on their own. Now they rarely visit or have anything to do with their father.

The only one who has stuck by him over the long run has

been his wife. And she has been the one to bear most of his bullying. She doesn't have the courage to confront him about this, and he sees no need to change.

He is a classic controlling man. Of course, not all men are like him, but many of us have some compulsion to control others.

When a man and a woman ride together in a car, who drives? I don't have statistics on this, but my experience and observation tell me that the man usually drives. I would guess it's 80 to 90 percent of the time. Would you agree?

I believe it's a control issue. Men like to be in control, and women don't mind not being in control.

I believe this desire to control others has several sources, including testosterone, social conditioning, and what I call religious expansion.

Drive for Accomplishment

First, the biological root of this tendency toward control may be the testosterone-propelled drive for accomplishment. As we have already seen, men are doers. Those who are most motivated to get something done will enlist others in the task. In essence, they will control themselves and others as they drive toward their goal. The goal itself really controls those who work toward it.

Women exert a different kind of control. Being more relationship oriented, women tend to seek a broader-based control: "Is this what everyone wants to do?"

Social Conditioning

Second, our society has layers and layers of conditioning for male control. For centuries, men have taken control and kept women from controlling things. So, when we say, "Men like to be in control," we're only telling half the story.

Everyone likes to be in control; it's just that women have been forced to learn how *not* to be in control.

Author Judith Segal writes about Testosterone Deference Syndrome, in which women regularly grant control to men. According to Segal, women learn to give in to men's wishes, to give men more respect than they give other women, to defer to men's authority in many needless ways. And we're not talking only about wives and husbands. Women in general defer to men in general. Segal wants her readers to recognize how they are doing that and to stop doing that.[2]

But men also learn to be take-charge guys, even if they are more submissive by nature. I have talked with a number of shy men who feel trapped by the age-old courting ritual of men asking women out on dates. Why must men always initiate the situation?

I've talked with other single gentlemen who are indeed gentle. Yet they may find themselves victimized by the nice guy syndrome. Some women complain about men who seek to control them, and yet they gravitate toward them. A truly gentle man does not radiate masculinity, and so these women aren't as attracted to him. They run after the users, the abusers, the controllers. What kind of image of masculinity do we have?

Religious Expansion

Some will say, "Aren't men supposed to be in control? Didn't God ordain it that way?" This is a touchy issue, one that we need to steer carefully through. Some Christians believe that the Bible mandates male authority in every aspect of life.

The Bible has specific teachings regarding male and female roles in the home and the church. These teachings are interpreted in different ways, but the New Testament does call the husband the "head" of the wife, just as Christ is the head of the church (Eph. 5:23). Is that a position of control? The apostle Paul urged husbands to love their wives "as Christ also loved the church and gave Himself for her" (Eph. 5:25). Whatever else headship entails, it certainly involves a sacrificial love and a giving spirit.

Some Christians have looked only at the surface of biblical teaching regarding men and women, and they have drawn false conclusions. This is what I call religious expansion. It takes a valid religious idea and expands its application until it is no longer valid. Thus some men claim authority based on the surface teaching of Scripture.

Others have the idea that all women must be subservient to all men. That is, women should not be managers in business, they should not seek political office, and they should not lead church committees. I believe they base these beliefs on the specific teachings about home and church, but they expand their application far beyond what's right. The biblical examples of Deborah as judge and Priscilla as counselor indicate that women can legitimately take control of situations.

Still, some men have a hard time working for a female boss. They feel it is somehow unspiritual for them to submit to women—in any context. I believe these men are exercising their basic desire for control and finding support in their expanded religious ideas.

Loss of Control

As men grow up, they gain increasing control of their lives and then the world around them. A man may have to pay his dues, serving others at his job, but his eye is set on advancement. He will soon be commanding others.

Even if it's not a line of direct authority, men soon discover their sphere of influence. They recognize their power over certain people and certain situations. Maybe that's why men like machines so much—machines do what you tell them. And what's the favorite household gadget for many men? The remote control. Push a button and you control the box across the room.

But what happens when men lose control? Presidents and other elected officials who have been voted out of office tell of a depression that sets in. They don't have the power they once had. What they say doesn't matter anymore. For many men, a midlife crisis occurs when they realize the limits of their power. They break free by doing something totally out of character and totally out of control. They abandon all to live in a beach hut. It's often a desperate attempt to regain control.

Older men are greatly frustrated by their loss of control. The pattern reverses. They were going up the ladder, but now they're headed down. They are demoted or downscaled or perhaps given a golden parachute and cut loose (or cut loose without any parachute at all). Do they matter anymore? The loss of control has emasculated them.

I know a man in his seventies who regularly complains about his personal loss of power. He can't do the things he used to do, and it makes him mad. "I put up this wall here," he says. "Now I can't even drive a nail into it." Many of us, in some way, can relate to the heartbreak of the aging process. But this heartbreak is very different for men and women. For men, it is largely an issue of control. When they lose control, even over their bodies, they wonder what good they are.

Relationships of the Rock

How does this need to control affect men's relationships? It depends whether we're talking about relationships with men or women, with other would-be controllers or people who are willing to be controlled.

Relationships with Men

I'm told that dogs have a pack mentality. They are very conscious of where they rank in relation to the other dogs in the pack. Training a dog can involve wrestling it down to establish the fact that you, as a human, have a higher rank. As long as the dog thinks it outranks you, it will not do what you say.

Men are like dogs. (Some of you women are agreeing with that too enthusiastically.) Men also have a pack mentality. When we are with other men, we have a sense of where we rank within the pack. It may not be at the forefront of our minds, but it's at least in the subconscious.

If we were all in the military, there would be stars and chevrons on our shoulders to proclaim our ranks. In real life, we have to win our place. That's where our competitive tendencies, as previously discussed, come into play. Among controllers, there's a constant one-upmanship—sometimes in the form of mild gibes, sometimes serious insults, sometimes games, sometimes fights.

Butting heads also occurs in real life as men face off for control of a work situation, a social situation, perhaps even a family situation. (As you may know, it can also happen between a man and a woman, but we'll get to that later.) Sometimes this confrontation is a fistfight, but many other less-violent power plays can occur. When two would-be controllers butt heads, one wins and the other loses. Or both lose. But at least one has to back down. The loser either submits to the control of the winner or leaves the scene. That's the way the pack works.

Men often develop parallel ranking in a relationship. A respects B for his expertise in certain areas, and B respects A for his ability in different areas. We choose particular provinces to control and let others control the rest.

Parallel ranking also occurs with united goals. In fact, the strongest male friendships arise among coworkers or teammates. We allow ourselves to share control of a situation because we share a common purpose. From time to time, subtle power plays may occur if we disagree on how to achieve our goals. But in general, the shared vision lets us cooperate.

In other cases, men yield control to others but maintain a quiet dissent: "I'll go along with this, but I won't like it." In governments, in businesses, and in churches, there are always people with minority views. They may not control what goes on, but they maintain control of their opinions. This happens not only in groups but also in relationships. If I realize I have no control over you, I may voice my dissent and then withdraw in some way. Many fathers do this with wayward sons or daughters.

Some controllers decide to yield to other controllers. There's the classic exchange: "You're fired!" "You can't fire me; I quit!" Controllers accept a situation beyond their control but redefine it so that it was their idea all along.

Relationships with Women

Understand that not all men are heavy controllers. In relationships with other men, some guys are happy to play second fiddle. The pack mentality allows men to identify with the leader of the pack and the rest of the pack, and maintain a level of self-respect even if they're not calling all the shots. But when women enter the picture, the entire situation changes. The need for control gets bumped up a notch or two. Guys who regularly give in to other guys suddenly develop a need to control the women in their lives. Moderate controllers from the male pack become high controllers with women. And high controllers become domineering.

Women often complain, "Why can't men be more honest

and open about their feelings?" We've already talked about men's relative lack of verbal ability. But another key issue here is control. We fear that if we open up, we may reveal that we are really not in control—at least not as much as we pretend to be.

That control may be small (unilaterally deciding what the family does on weekends) or great (prohibiting a wife from leaving the house on her own). In the smaller cases, it is often a matter of role playing. The man feels that this control is expected of him. He doesn't know any other way. He is often a blinded controller, not realizing the effects of his domination. Thorough communication can often bring such a man to share control more easily.

But I have seen situations where a husband made his wife sever all her friendships. He insisted on certain behavior in the home. He grilled her about her daily activities and kept her self-esteem low through regular insults. In some cases, physical abuse was involved.

I hope you are not in such an extreme situation. But you probably deal with control issues in your relationship. It seems that it should be so easy—two grown adults deciding things together. But remember that men regularly see things in terms of rank. We are always keeping score. We see a way to get something done, and we want to push the buttons to do it.

If you women get in the way (by having your own ideas), we feel (*a*) frustrated because the buttons aren't as easy to push; (*b*) insulted because you don't trust our judgment (never mind that we seldom trust your judgment); and (*c*) insecure because we feel our control slipping away, and that's a central part of our role (and identity) within the relationship—if we aren't in control, who are we?

How do men solve control issues in the male pack? We went through several methods earlier. You may adapt some of them to your situation. (You may be doing this already.)

- Butting heads. It's not the best way, but sometimes it's the only way to get through. State your opinions and your absolute desire for shared control.
- Dividing the spoils. You balance the checkbook; I'll buy the groceries. I trust your expertise there; you trust mine here.
- United goals. Agree on a general direction for your lives together, and set broad parameters for your day-to-day decisions.
- Quiet dissent. If he gets his way, over your objection, let it happen. Go along as much as you can, but withdraw as much as you need to. Don't sabotage his plans, and please fight the temptation to say, "I told you so."
- Decide to yield. You may decide to adopt his idea as your own—not as a power play but as a genuine attempt to cooperate. Understand that he may decide to yield and maintain his control by claiming credit for your plan.

Relationships with Children

Some traits common to men—their nonverbality and goal orientation—can have a devastating effect on their children, especially daughters. I've counseled a number of women and a few men who are much like Jane Fonda's character in the movie *On Golden Pond*. They are still trying to win their fathers' approval. They may be miles away; they may not have spoken for years. In some cases the fathers are dead, but the adult children long for that hard-won praise from dear old dad.

There's a memorable scene in the movie *The Great Santini* in which the sassy teenage daughter literally begs for attention from her military father. She knows she won't get it, so she plays it for laughs, yet the scene has an underlying poignancy.

The father reads the paper as the daughter says she wants to talk. He ignores her. As the scene progresses, she kneels before him, grabs his legs, and says, "Let's bare our souls and get to know one another."

"I don't want you to get to know me," he snarls from behind the paper. "I like being an enigma." Then he stalks away.

Through criticism, punishment, and silence, men develop control over their children that may last a lifetime. Some men don't realize the effect they have. Other men do, and they enjoy their power. Some don't know any other way to be.

It must be one of the hardest things anyone has to do, to lose control of a child, to watch the child grow up into independent adulthood. Many do not make the transition gracefully. Many fathers never completely give up their control. In such cases, they miss out on what could be deeply fulfilling adult-adult relationships—and they threaten to ruin the lives of their adult children by holding on too tightly.

Relationships with God

Men's desire for control makes it more difficult to establish a deep relationship with God.

A key element of Christianity is submission. Jesus Christ submitted to the Cross (Phil. 2:6–8). Christians are to submit to one another (Eph. 5:21). When we are hit, Jesus said, we should stand there and let ourselves be hit again (Matt. 5:39). If you want to be a leader, be a servant (Mark 10:42–45). The meek inherit the earth (Matt. 5:5). If you are into control, all of this is hard to take.

The man who loves control has difficulty surrendering all to God. If he's used to making his own decisions, it won't be easy to let God call the shots.

Some Christian men use many of the same strategies we've already discussed. Some butt heads with God. I think of Jacob being wrestled down, like a dog, and getting his hip thrown out of joint (Gen. 32:22–32).

If you are pulling your man into greater church involvement or a deeper spiritual life, and he's dragging his feet, it may not be the preacher or the hymns or even the theology that he really objects to. Those may be smokescreens. It may be the issue of control. It's hard for such a man to let go.

Chapter Eight

I Am an Island

Simon and Garfunkel sang about an emotional recluse, someone who was hurt once and now withdraws from relationships. It's not so dramatic with most men, yet there is a tendency to keep others at arm's length. Even if he does enter relationships, the independent man tends to keep them at a surface level.

They tell me that there is a resurgence in the popularity of the classic Western movie. But these are really not about the West. Their themes are more along the lines of one man, the lone cowboy, pitted against all odds, who overcomes evil and wins the heart of the heroine. It's a hackneyed story, but it still sells. Let's not kid ourselves into thinking that the role of men in our society is much more enlightened today.

CHARACTERISTIC #7: MEN LIKE TO FEEL INDEPENDENT

This is the legend of the American cowboy: a proud, independent man, who can withstand long periods of time in complete isolation, enduring all hardships, with never a whisper of complaint. The only thing a good cowboy would complain about would be being tied down. "Keep moving and stay aloof" would be his motto.

So it is with many men. We have an independent spirit, which is part of our history and heritage. If women are viewed as being weak and dependent, men must strive to be the opposite.

Origins

Where does this independent spirit come from? I believe there may be some biological basis in our testosterone-induced aggression and goal orientation. The task is more important than the relationship. While other people can help us achieve the task, they often get in the way. If you want it done right, do it yourself.

But as with most of these gender distinctions we've been discussing, independence is also a matter of social conditioning. The cowboy spirit is deeply ingrained in our culture. Our heroes ride alone.

If you bristled when you read, a few paragraphs ago, about women being viewed as weak and dependent, good. Certainly, women are not necessarily that way, and dependence does not have to be weak. But that is the understanding most of us have grown up with. Girls learn to find strength in relationships. That in itself is a positive thing, but boys learn to turn that around.

Warren T. Farrell, describing a study of elementary school textbooks, summarizes a common attitude found in them: "In order to be a real boy, a boy must not be caught being at all like a girl." This attitude, he says, increases as boys grow older.[1]

Another factor in the development of independence among boys, I think, is our wounding. Boys get hurt in relationships. Perhaps they're betrayed by a best buddy, or maybe it's the pain of preadolescent unrequited love. Kids can be cruel—they're all learning about relationships—and that can cause pain.

Girls get hurt as much as boys do, but girls heal better. Girls cry. Girls talk. Girls find support from others. Boys don't do any of those things as easily, and so their pain festers. They become like the unfortunate character in the Simon and Garfunkel song. They forswear friendship, at least deep friendship. They build their fortresses so they won't be hurt again.

Then as they grow, the independence produces a vicious cycle of pain and new withdrawal. If they do venture out of their fortress and get hurt again, they have no support system to help them. They have no way to heal.

My experiences leading seminars for people who have gotten divorces have heightened my awareness of this male tendency. Who gets divorced—men or women? Both! And in approximately even numbers. But who comes to these seminars to get help? Overwhelmingly, women. Do men sustain less pain from divorce? Maybe a little. I suppose more women are victimized in divorces, but not that many more. It seems to be this male independence at work. Men are more reluctant to seek help, even if they are hurting badly.

"Not Good"

In the creation account in the book of Genesis, God works for six days making the earth and everything in it. At the end of each day, He looks at His handiwork and calls it "good." Soon afterward, there is something He calls "not good." Do you know what it is?

"It is not good that man should be alone," God says (Gen. 2:18). That, of course, led to the creation of Eve.

Some have taken this statement to mean that God wants everyone to be married. I don't believe that. (See 1 Cor. 7:32–38.) But it is clear that utter independence is "not good." Fiercely independent men can live lonely and emotionally isolated lives.

Relationships of the Island

How does our desire for independence affect our relationships? Obviously, the most severely independent person will withdraw from all relationships, but few men are that independent. Most independent men develop functional friendships.

Friendships with Men

Our independence causes our relationships with men to be more a matter of convenience than of commitment. I would never decide that I need to get together with Bill. No, we might plan to do something together that we both enjoyed, but the activity would be the main event, not the friendship.

Surely, there are exceptions. Some men have forged deep friendships that they regularly cultivate. But most male friends observe an unspoken code: Don't get too close.

Relationships with Women

How does this tendency toward independence affect our relationships with women? Well, it keeps us out of those relationships, or it creates problems within them.

It has been said that "men fall basically into two categories, the cowboy or the playboy."[2] We have already discussed the cowboy some, so let's talk about the playboy.

"The playboy," writes counselor James E. Kilgore,

> is rarely satisfied with *one* woman and constantly in search of something more—that elusive woman who will fulfill

> his fantasy! He places little value on any woman in particular and is unable to make a genuine commitment to one. He notices every woman, is intrigued by her uniqueness, and in his own way he needs to find a special place in the life of every woman he knows.[3]

Playboys are dangerous because they seem to pay a lot of attention to women. They learn to woo women well. Though they may not make any verbal promises, everything they do seems to be heading toward a wonderful relationship. But make no mistake—they do this for their own benefit. The wooing is focused not on the woman but on the playboy. A playboy proves his value every time he dates a desirable woman. Or so he thinks.

The playboy is on a quest—maybe for his sexual pleasure but not necessarily. That's what's so disarming. A playboy may be on a quest for the perfect relationship. He may be seeking that fantasy woman. Ultimately, he is seeking himself. It is that independent spirit coming through strongly. A woman may help him along on his journey, but if she isn't the ideal woman (and who is?), she is easily scuttled. Any sort of commitment to a less-than-ideal woman would be a major compromise on his quest. He would be signing away a major part of himself. He would be giving up his independence.

The cowboy may commit to a relationship, even a marriage, but he remains directed outward. A frontier out there somewhere must be tamed. The loving wife may be there when he returns from riding the range. He may stop for the night to rest his horse and get some good lovin', but soon he's out on the range again.

The "range" may be different for every man. It's his independent activity. For many men, it's the job. They work nine to nine, and then at home they're still noodling some problem. For others, it's a hobby, a sport, a church activity, or even an affair. Whatever it is, their energy is directed outward, and they tend to shut other people out.

If you are the loving wife, you may try to capture the cowboy's attention. You may strive to be a part of his activity, to ride the range with him, but even that's a disappointment because his eyes are always on the horizon. You're just an extra appendage.

There's a bit of the cowboy in every man. We need to go off by ourselves and gaze at the stars every so often. But a couple need to find a balance. With wise negotiation, independence and interdependence can coexist.

Let's return to the image of the cave. Men tend to withdraw into themselves, especially in stressful situations. At the very times when women need to talk things over, men go off by themselves. "When a man is stressed he will withdraw into the cave of his mind and focus on solving a problem," writes John Gray. "He becomes so focused on solving this one problem that he temporarily loses awareness of everything else. . . . At such times, he becomes increasingly distant, forgetful, unresponsive, and preoccupied in his relationships."[4]

Male independence can be maddening. It can be damaging (as with the playboy), inconsiderate (as with the cowboy), and mysterious (as in the cave). But for a man, in proper measure, it can be restorative and energizing.

The man who goes off by himself is not necessarily being selfish, nor is the woman who insists on talking when he is reading the paper. Both have needs, and you may require creativity in finding ways to meet both sets of needs.

Chapter Nine

Me, Myself, and I

Rob Becker has uncovered a great truth about the sexes. It has to do with potato chips.

In a group of women, if the chip bowl is low, they "will all get up and move to get more." There is something instinctual within them that seeks to meet the need of the group. "It's a very cooperative thing," Becker says. "They won't even stop the conversation."

But men are totally different. If the chip bowl is running low, "they will break into negotiation. One guy says, 'I bought the chips.' Another says, 'I put them in the bowl.' And still another says, 'It's my bowl.' And they will go on until somebody doesn't have anything to bargain with, and he has to get the chips."

Becker has a ninety-minute comedy routine, "Defending the Caveman," that's knocking 'em dead in various cities of the U.S. But it's more than comedy; it's anthropology, sociology, and psychology, all celebrating the differences between the sexes. "We all know instinctively we are different," he says. "My show is one way to understand the differences that empower both sexes."

Problems occur when people ignore or deny the differences. Becker says that most fights between the sexes are "misunderstandings based on a clash of two cultures, languages, histories."[1]

Take the chip thing. The men's negotiations are based on a male desire for fairness and self-assertion. The women's behavior is based on a female ideal of service to the group. But in mixed company, if the chips are low and a man says, "Somebody get more chips; I bought them," the women think he's an incredibly selfish jerk.

According to their rules, he's being selfish. But he's playing by the male rules of fair distribution of labor. The two rule books are different and encourage vastly different behaviors. To men, women often seem like spineless jellyfish, never standing up for themselves. To women, men often seem like selfish pigs.

CHARACTERISTIC #8: MEN TEND TO HAVE A STRONGER SELF-FOCUS

Let me remind you that we're dealing in generalities.

Authors Anne Moir and David Jessel cite research on male-female differences and conclude,

> Women can store, for short periods at least, more irrelevant and random information than men. Men can only manage the trick when the information is organized into some coherent form or has a specific *relevance to them.* So men are more self-centered—so what else is new? What's new is that the folklore of gender, which is always vulnerable to dismissive, politically motivated, fashionable opinion, is now shown to have a basis in scientific fact.[2]

Male hormone increases		*Female hormone decreases*
	AGGRESSION COMPETITION SELF-ASSERTION SELF-CONFIDENCE SELF-RELIANCE[3]	

In *Male and Female Realities*, Joe Tannenbaum points out the differences in male and female "ego strength." Men, he says, are more self-focused, while women are more other-focused. "A man's reality," Tannenbaum writes, "starts inside himself and moves outward." A man is the center of his own universe. That is not to say that men choose to put themselves at the center of the universe; it is just the way men think. Where men are "exclusive," women are "inclusive." Men find energy within themselves and expend it as they move out toward the world, while women find energy out there and expend it as they move in toward themselves.[4]

Male Focus	***Female Focus***
I	We
I act	We discuss
My world is ordered around me	Our world flows around us
I fight for my place in the world	We arrange ways of living together
I exert control over others	I seek to include others
I seek to have my needs met by others	I feel good when serving

You might say that men see the world by the measure of themselves, while women see themselves by the measure of the world. The self-focus of men affects several major areas of life, particularly awareness, self-assurance, and selfish behavior.

Awareness

HE: What's the matter?

SHE: You know.

HE: Know what?

SHE: Don't act innocent with me. You know exactly what you did.

HE: No, really. Tell me what's the matter.

SHE: If you really loved me, you'd know. When you're ready to apologize, then I'll talk to you again. Otherwise, I've got nothing more to say.

Have you ever had a conversation like this? I have.

Women are always tuning in to events outside themselves. Women gather information and sort through it, turning it around like a kaleidoscope. So women are often aware of men's needs before men are.

Conflict arises, however, when men and women assume they're playing by the same rules. As in the conversation just cited, women can assume that men are as perceptive as women are. And a basic rule in the female rule book is: "If you see that someone you love has a problem, ask how you can help." When a man (1) doesn't see the problem and (2) doesn't offer to help, a woman can assume that he doesn't care.

But the male rule book, based on the principle of male independence, reads: "Don't meddle. If someone needs something, he'll ask." So, if you have a problem, your man may assume that you can handle it; thus, it's not his problem. You may be in the kitchen, being eaten alive by the garbage disposal while your husband reads the paper. But unless you ask for help directly—"Honey, I need your help NOW!"—he won't hear you.

Awareness is also an issue when marriage partners deal with the outside world. My wife is more likely to notice when someone else is in need. And she's much more likely to want to do something about that need.

SHE: We should really do more to help with Habitat for Humanity. Why don't we call and see if we can volunteer for this weekend?

HE: Uh, I've got a golf game this weekend.

SHE: But this is for a good cause.

HE: There will be other good causes to come along. They always do.

In this scenario, it's not really selfishness we're seeing on the part of the man, just a self-focus. Men tend to go through life with a kind of tunnel vision. Women have Cinemascope.

Self-Assurance

I wrote a book with Randy Petersen about addictive relationships called *Love Gone Wrong*. In interviewing people for the book and citing examples from my counseling, we found a common thread: low self-esteem. We also found that the great majority of relationship-addicted people were women.

So we wrote a book on self-esteem called *Becoming Your Own Best Friend*, and once again we found that our examples were mostly women. Again and again, we ran across women of great ability, intelligence, and attractiveness putting themselves down. They felt they were not good enough.

And though I have encountered some men with low self-esteem, I know many others who seem to think too highly of themselves. You've met these guys, too. Some of them, to be sure, are masking deep insecurities. But I'm convinced that most of them genuinely think they're better than they really are. It galls me that there are women ten times smarter and more talented who get intimidated by the bluster of these guys.

The biological basis for this inequity may be the self-focus of our brains. But there is certainly a cultural force at work here, too. Our society has been skewed toward men in many ways. The last quarter century has seen some changes, but an imbalance remains. From earliest upbringing, boys are taught to like being male, and girls get the message that they're not as good.

For years, Judith Segal taught graduate courses in human sexuality. Each year, she gave a survey, asking the women to list the messages they got about how girls and women are and how boys and men should be.

Segal says that year after year, the same descriptions came up. Women got the message that they were "money spenders, not moneymakers," "here to make people happy," "not supposed to talk back," "not supposed to get angry," "not supposed to let boys know that they're smart," "bad drivers," "naive," and "fickle." There were many more, but you get the idea.

These women also got the message that males should be "superior to women," "stronger," "smarter," "confident," "financially secure," "demanding," and so on.

Then Segal asked the men in her classes to list messages about how boys and men are and how girls and women should be. They got the message that boys and men are "rough," "tough," "good lovers," "selfish," "unemotional," "competitive," "mechanically inclined," "domineering," "unfaithful," and more.

They also got the message that females should be "shorter than boys," "soft-spoken," "naive," "graceful," "slim," "maternal," "faithful," "subservient," "good cooks," and so on.[5]

You could probably make a similar list. The point is that girls get the message that they are of secondary importance: "Don't outshine the boys." All of the comments in the lists—from men and women—regularly show the females in relation to the males. Girls learn to adjust to that.

All of this makes childhood a factory for low female self-esteem. Studies have shown that teachers tend to pay more attention to boys. Girls understate their ability so they won't show up the boys. Many high schools throw great enthusiasm (and money) into boys' sports and less into girls' sports. Other departments that are largely populated by girls, such as music, drama, and art, are often ignored.

Yes, schools are different now from when you and I grew up. There is more attention to equality of treatment for both sexes. Maybe this will do some good. But meanwhile, we have generations of grown men who are pretty sure of themselves and grown women who think they're not so good.

Most men, especially men who love too little, don't realize how the system has hampered the success of women. They assume the world is a rather just place, and people get what they deserve.

But men and women don't have to be opposed on the self-esteem issue. If they work as a team, they can balance each other. A woman with low self-esteem can bring some realism to a bragging man. A man with self-confidence can encourage and empower a self-doubting woman.

Two dangers can derail you. The first is worship, or what you might call person addiction. Sometimes a woman begins to believe that her man can do no wrong and (with her low self-esteem) that she can do nothing right. He may ignore her for days on end, which she accepts because she feels unworthy of his attention anyway. It becomes a zero-sum game of personal worth. If he's worth more, she's worth less. That's a very unhealthy situation.

A second potential problem, which is more common, is personality warfare. Sometimes a woman with low self-esteem will be jealous of her man's high self-esteem, so she'll try to drag him down to her level. She points out every instance where he's wrong or ignorant or failing. She essentially forces him into a defensive position, which makes him appear even more conceited. Every discussion becomes an attack. This, too, is unhealthy. No one can win these battles.

Instead, try to cultivate a situation in which you both can laugh at yourselves. If he can laugh at his swagger and you at your humility, you'll be fine.

Selfish Behavior

If I am not aware of the needs of others, I can do selfish things without realizing it: "Oh, why didn't you remind me that it was our anniversary? I wouldn't have worked late."

If I consider my needs more important than the needs of others, I can do selfish things but feel justified in doing them: "I'm too tired to have Betty and Joe over tonight. Why don't you call them and reschedule?"

In such cases, my normal male self-focus is turning into selfish behavior. I am choosing to keep my focus narrow. Thanks to my wife, my awareness has been stretched to include the needs and concerns of others. But if I still put my needs first, I am being selfish.

The apostle Paul wrote to the Philippians, "Let nothing be done through selfish ambition or conceit, but in lowliness of mind let each esteem others better than himself. *Let each of you look out not only for his own interests, but also for the interests of others*" (Phil. 2:3–4, emphasis added). I maintain that it is harder for men than for women to follow this teaching. We have a natural tendency toward "selfish ambition" and "conceit." And we find it hard to look beyond our interests.

Levels of Selfishness

It might help, though, to consider levels of selfish attitudes and behavior. All of us, men and women, can be selfish to some extent, yet there's a wide range of selfishness, from merely self-focused to narcissistic. At one end of this continuum, it's a fairly benign situation. A couple should be able to work things out with proper communication. At the other end, it's a clinical problem. The serious narcissist needs help if he'll accept it.

Both men and women can fluctuate along this continuum, depending on their moods, how their day is going, and who they are relating to. Joe Tannenbaum presents a pattern, sort of an ebb and flow, in which men expend energy as we move out to deal with the world, then we retreat within ourselves to restore our energy. Women have a similar pattern, except the energy flow is reversed.[6] So, our awareness and focus at any given time may depend on whether we're moving out toward the world or retreating from it.

As we have seen, men have a greater self-focus and therefore a greater tendency toward selfish behavior. Our need to control, our independence, and our logic combine to make us more self-aware, self-reliant, self-focused, and probably more self-centered.

Part 2

Types of Men Who Love Too Little

Chapter Ten

The Angry Man

Jack had come home from work in a foul mood. And when nine-year-old Robbie ran into the living room playing ray gun with the electric drill, Jack lost control. It was not the first time Robbie had played with his father's tools—he knew it was wrong. But this time Jack did not scold the boy or send him to his room. Instead, Jack got violent.

In the middle of the scene, Sue hurried into the room. She begged her husband to stop, then tried to restrain him. She knew from experience that Jack's outburst would soon subside.

Jack stopped and stormed into the kitchen. Sue took her son in her arms and carried him to his room, whispering words of comfort. She knew what she had to do.

THE ULTIMATUM

It wasn't until bedtime, however, when she delivered her ultimatum. After avoiding her for most of the evening, Jack found Sue reading in bed. Sensing her displeasure, he launched a half-hearted apology: "I guess I was a little hard on Robbie. But he's got to learn to obey me. He needs to learn some respect."

Sue gazed in disbelief. She told him, "You don't get it, do you? It's not Robbie. It's you. You have a problem with your temper. And if you don't get some professional help, well, you may come home someday and find that Robbie and I aren't here."

Within the week, he called for a counseling appointment, but he wasn't convinced that he had a problem. As he saw it, the problems were around him.

A NATURAL RESPONSE

Everyone gets angry. It's a fact of life. Some feel mild annoyance; others burst with intense rage. Some men who love too little make anger a habit. It's as if they look for occasions to fly off the handle. In dealing with men like this—men like Jack—we need to understand the nature of anger, the good and the bad of it.

Anger can be destructive—unresolved anger can lead to ongoing bitterness, depression, low self-esteem, and marital conflict. Yet anger is not, in and of itself, wrong. Essentially, it is *a natural response to a perceived injustice*.

The key word in this definition is *perceived*. When you think someone else has done you wrong, you respond with anger. But you might also feel anger toward a neighborhood bully who is picking on little kids. An injustice is occurring, and you feel the wrongness of it. So anger is not necessarily selfish, although our basic sense of self-preservation often skews our sense of justice.

We are all Solomons, you might say, judging the situations

of our lives and determining who's right and who's wrong. Some people have the ability to withhold judgment, to give others the benefit of the doubt, to avoid finding fault. These people don't get angry as often. But those who are constantly judging the situations of their lives will feel angry when they think something is going wrong.

When we view it like that, we see that the anger impulse is basically a desire for justice. As such, it is a very good thing. Many of us applaud the righteous indignation of someone who speaks out against hunger in Somalia or genocide in Bosnia or racism in the U.S. These are righteous causes, and the anger that goes with them is fueled by this desire to see justice prevail.

But all anger is righteous indignation, at least to that angry person at that time. Even the most selfish person, when angry, is responding to a situation in which he feels he is being wronged. He desires justice for himself, and he will act violently, if need be, to get it.

THE PROBLEM WITH ANGER

The main problem with anger, of course, is that our judgment is faulty. We frequently misjudge situations. We tend to place more importance on our needs than on the needs of others. We think we are being wronged when there is nothing really wrong.

Need inflation occurs regularly in romantic relationships and marriages—especially when there is a lack of communication. "Doesn't she understand that I need time to myself?" "Doesn't he understand that I need him here with me?" Both partners can simmer in an anger that seems righteous to them but suffers from faulty judgment.

A second problem with anger is misdirection. In our rush to find a culprit, we can quickly blame someone who is not at fault. We may act as judges of our situations, but we seldom take the time for a full trial. Instead, we lash out at anyone who's nearby.

Misdirection happens frequently in marriages. A man may be mad at his boss or his brother or his baseball team, but his wife bears the brunt of it. She's there. Naturally, she may respond with righteous anger of her own, and the home becomes a war zone because of something that has nothing to do with the marital relationship.

A third problem with anger is that it often grows out of proportion to the problem. Anger is a fire. In proper measure, it can burn the leaves from your backyard. But unless it is wisely tended, it may burn all the trees and houses in your neighborhood. The impulse may be righteous in some way, just as a match may be struck for some very good reasons, but the expression of anger often burns out of control. The biblical command makes sense: "Be angry, and do not sin" (Eph. 4:26). That anger will occur is assumed, but be careful about the things it makes you do.

Another problem with anger is what it does to the angry person. Ideally, anger is felt, expressed (or resolved), and done away with. But it seldom works that way.

In recent years, we have heard a great deal about the repression of anger and how unhealthy that is. Repression turns the energy of anger inward, causing physical stress, emotional bitterness, and spiritual dryness. When a person bottles up angry feelings inside, the feelings eat away at his attitude, his relationships, and his body. The physical stress caused by the repression of angry feelings can cause or exacerbate such problems as high blood pressure, heart disease, fatigue, poor digestion, ulcers, and skin disease.

It has been fashionable for counselors to urge clients to let out their anger. The way to combat the scourge of repressed anger is to express it, they say. To a point, this is true. But some have taken this advice too far. They end up encouraging anger. As a person gets used to expressing his anger, he may become more angry, taking offense at every little thing.

In general, expression is better than repression (although we may have to choose carefully the time and place). But it's even better to deal with anger by going back to its roots—the perception of what's right and wrong in our situations, the expectations of justice, even our honest appraisal of ourselves.

JACK'S SESSION

Jack walked into my office and looked around, inspecting the premises. He sat down in front of me with an I-dare-you-to-help-me look. Sunk back in his chair, arms crossed, this twentysomething husband and father reminded me of many teenagers I've counseled.

As our hour of counseling drew to a close, it became apparent to me that Jack had suffered a pattern of physical, emotional, and verbal abuse as a boy. His anger went all the way back to his childhood. As a result, he had little patience in his parenting. His low level of frustration tolerance was directly related to his childhood abuse. Would Jack ever come to grips with his anger and realize that it was damaging his relationships with those he loved?

I gave him the Fitzgibbons Anger Inventory, asked him to fill it out, and bring it back to his next session. This self-test is a useful indicator of anger levels. If Jack would answer the questions honestly, it would help him to see how angry he really was. Perhaps seeing it in black and white would help him to realize how his anger was affecting his family. At least that was my hope.

THE REASONS

Why is anger more of a problem for men than for women? Do men get angry more often? Are they provoked more often? Do they stay angry longer? Or do they channel their anger in less-helpful ways? Perhaps all of the above.

1. *Men's heightened sense of self skews their perception of justice.* Throughout this book, we're speaking in generalities, but we saw in chapter 9 that men tend to have a stronger sense of self than women do. When we plug that fact into our understanding of anger as a response to perceived injustice, it follows that men feel wronged more often.

Women are taught to downplay their needs for the good of the family or society in general. Men are taught to fight for what they want.

2. *Anger can help to achieve the goals of men but not of women.* The big football game is coming up. The newspaper reports that the Lions' players have been saying bad things about the Bears. What does the Bears' coach do? He clips the article, highlights the quotes, and posts it in the Bears' locker room. Why? To get the guys riled up. Anger gets the adrenaline going, and that means greater intensity out on the field. It will give the Bears a competitive edge.

Life is a football game for a lot of men. They work in highly competitive situations, or they make a competition out of everything. Winning is the only thing for these men, and they'll do whatever it takes—including getting angry enough to get pumped up to win.

In our society, anger often works for men, and it backfires on women. Angry women are seen as shrill and unreasonable. Angry men are often seen as driven, directed, inspired. In this split-level world, women learn that they have to channel their anger into more productive behavior that accomplishes their more relational goals. Men don't learn that. As long as anger works, men will get angry.

3. *Men's lack of verbal skills keeps them from venting their anger in healthy ways.* The book of Proverbs says, "A soft answer turns away wrath" (15:1). Why? Because a soft answer begins the process of resolution. If you have a complaint against me, let's talk. Let's see who's at fault. If it's my mistake, what can I do to make it better? Suddenly, the rug is pulled out from under the feet of anger.

But men tend to have difficulty with soft answers. I have counseled a number of abusive men who cannot argue with their wives. That is, their wives are far more verbal and thus always win. These men cannot express their ideas nearly as well, and so they resort to violence, relying on their physical superiority to prove their points.

This nonverbality does not always come out in violent anger; it often results in a seething frustration.

Why not talk about it? Why let the annoyance fester? It all goes back to a general lack of verbal expression among men. This can contribute in a big way to the problem of anger.

4. *Men's desire for control causes frequent frustration.* If I am driving on the Schuylkill Expressway through Philadelphia on my way to an important meeting, and suddenly there's a traffic tie-up, I get frustrated. There's nothing I can do to go any faster. Things are out of my control. I hate that feeling. Sometimes I have taken the next exit, gotten myself hopelessly lost, and ended up at the meeting even later than I would have if I had stayed on the expressway. But at least I took control of my situation.

Maybe there was a time when men could consider themselves fully in control of their lives and their families, but times have changed. We are troubled by terrorism, taxes, layoffs, computerization, liberated women, unruly children, planned obsolescence, hurricanes, health care costs, and an information superhighway with an MTV speed limit. When we're honest, there's not a whole lot that we can control. But we try. And that causes frustration, which steeps for a while and then erupts into anger.

Women learned a long time ago that control is a group thing. We must learn to work with others and roll with the tides. This Christian teaching is often overlooked: The way to lead is to serve (Mark 10:42–45).

All of these issues—sense of self, competitive spirit, lack of verbal skills, and desire for control—were at work in Jack's case. Sue needed to learn how to deal with it all.

"A STONE WALL BETWEEN US"

"How are you doing?" I asked Sue in a separate session.

"I don't know," she sighed. "I'm losing hope."

"What has it been like for you, living with Jack?"

Sue stared out the window, searching for her response. "I've tried, I really have. But his anger is like a stone wall between us. I mean, I just can't love him if he won't let me. And every time I feel his anger, it's as if he's screaming, 'Stay away!' How can you have a marriage with someone like that?"

After eleven years of angry outbursts, occurring almost weekly, Sue was desperately hurting. Jack's anger seemed to be contagious. She found herself throwing temper tantrums, and she could see what Jack's brutality was doing to their son.

"What changed?" I asked. "What made you finally decide to come for help?"

"I just couldn't take it anymore," she replied. "I want Jack to admit his anger, to deal with it, and to stop abusing our boy. Can you help him? Is that too much to ask?"

HEALING HER HURTS

A man's problem with anger can take a terrible toll on the woman who loves him. Sue was dealing with it as best she could, but it was a struggle. Compounding her distress was her concern for her son. She feared for his physical safety and his emotional development.

What can a woman do in a situation like this? The prescription for healing in this book follows a pattern of understand, cope, and nudge. In the example, Sue follows this pattern well.

Understanding

It is crucial for Sue and others in her situation to understand that they are not to blame. The angry man sprays machine-gun fire around him; it hits everyone. He is hurting, and so he tries to hurt others. The angry man can say devastating things, things that damage a woman's self-esteem.

In such a case, the woman must shield herself with the understanding that "this is not my problem. I am not to blame."

With that basic understanding in place, the woman can begin to examine whether she does anything to spark or exacerbate the anger. This examination must be honest but reasonable. The angry man will tend to say it's all your fault. Do not believe him. Discuss the issue in nonangry moments. Consider getting an outside opinion from a trusted friend.

If anger is basically a natural response to a perceived injustice, try to determine what your man feels is unjust. Are you treating him unjustly, or does he think you are? How might this change?

There may be hidden issues. Remember that a man tends to clam up when a discussion gets close to how he really feels about important stuff. He will send smoke screens of trivia to keep you away.

If you try to talk about the hidden issues, do so in a non-threatening, nonattacking way. Be ready to listen, to consider, but do not give in to a guilt trip. Angry men are quick to dish out blame. If you accept the blame, you'll never get to the true issues. Remember, though, that a soft answer turns away wrath. If you begin to feel defensive, do not lash out in anger. Back off, if need be, and try the discussion some other time.

Coping

But how do you live with it? You may understand it, and that may help a little, but what if he never changes? How do you deal with an angry man who stays angry?

You must set up boundaries. This sounds like a step backward for the relationship, but establishing rules for the relationship is the only way to get it back on solid ground. What behavior will not be tolerated?

Sue came to that point when she stipulated that Jack's physical beating of their son had to stop. She could not put up with that behavior anymore. Many other women have drawn the line at personal violence—"If you hit me, we're through."

Another boundary you must set up is emotional. You must refuse to let yourself be drawn into the angry man's problems. Do not play the blame game, and do not return anger for anger. You have already offered your understanding and support, but your man is refusing to take steps toward health.

Coping with an angry man requires self-nourishment. Day after day you receive the bombardment of angry attacks from your man. Stop focusing on how to solve the problems of this angry man, and make sure your emotional needs are met. He may attack you for being selfish. He is on a sinking ship, and you've thrown him a dozen life preservers. Save yourself.

More than ever, you need a few close friends for support. You also need to make sure your spiritual life is on good footing. Pray often, bringing your needs before God. Your ordeal may make you feel unworthy of God, but be assured that He specializes in helping those who are hurting. Find spiritual strength in prayer, church, and Scripture.

Though the boundaries are important, keep sending out olive branches. Let your man know that peace is possible, but he needs to take some positive steps. If you are committed to this relationship, carve a door in that wall between you and put out a welcome mat. Let him know what he needs to do to restore a healthy relationship with you.

Nudging

Your boundary lines and olive branches may change his angry behavior, at least to a more tolerable level. Keep reasonable expectations throughout this process. You're not going to create a Gandhi. But you and your man may find ways to keep his anger under control.

Since anger is a natural response to a perceived injustice, one way to calm it is to modify perceptions. If a man believes life owes him a luxurious home, a fancy car, a high-level job, and perfect kids, he will be frustrated by reality. But if he modifies his perceptions of what he deserves, the frustration will be blunted.

If your man is constantly angry at injustices that he's blowing out of proportion, you may be able to talk through the issues at the expectation level: "What did you expect? What do you really think you deserve?" Often people interpret the comments or actions of others as personal attacks when they probably aren't meant that way. Perhaps you could suggest alternate interpretations: "Look at it through that person's eyes; he probably didn't mean any harm." As a nudger, take every opportunity to draw the angry person out of his narrow perception. Ask him to consider how justice might be done for others.

Anger often erupts where it shouldn't. Sometimes you can help the situation by redirecting the issue. If your man yells at you for buying the wrong brand of margarine, don't argue the point. He's probably steamed about something else. Talk about the real problem. Plead your innocence or that of your kids if he's picking on them. Call for justice. You don't deserve to be treated like this.

Anger often boils over, out of proportion to the problem at hand. That was Jack's problem with Robbie. Sue would have agreed that punishment was necessary. She would have been a bit angry with Robbie herself. But Jack's rage rose out of all proportion to the issue. In such cases, the nudger needs to hold a mirror up to the angry man: "Is this justice? Is this right? Are you responding appropriately? Are you in control, or is anger controlling you?" It needs to be done gently. It needs to be a calm call for self-appraisal. A man may be unaware of the effects of his anger. He needs to know how bad it gets.

The nudger also needs to seek out opportunities for healthy venting of anger. As a man goes through a day, the myriad frustrations pile up. Physically, the stress mounts—the body tightens, the heart races, the breath shortens. You can talk about the issues all you want, but a physical release is probably needed. Even if he doesn't join a gym, perhaps he could take walks or do deep-breathing exercises or put a punching bag in the basement. On another level, an activity might help him (or both of you) to do something really important. Lead a Scouting troop or host a church Bible study or tutor kids in the inner city. Any of these activities (and many others) might be an emotional vent for frustration and might bring the angry man out of his self-centered perspective.

Remember that *the man has to decide to change himself*. You cannot change him. Perhaps you can nudge him in the right direction, but he must choose to go that way.

Learn to use "I language." Talk about your needs and feelings, but don't call him names or analyze his motivations. Avoid saying, "You're out of control! You're just trying to hurt me! You have no feelings for your family!" Instead, try statements like these: "I hate it when you act this way. I can't live with you if you keep this up. It really hurts me to see you like this."

In this way, you are pulling him out of his self-focus, you are claiming the importance of your feelings, and you are reserving his right to make decisions about his life—you're just making it clear how his choices affect you.

Encourage him every time he comes close to handling his anger in a healthy way. If you say, "You never . . . ," or "You always . . . ," he will have no motivation to change. But if you compliment him more, he may be more accepting when you point out an area that needs work.

GETTING HELP

As with most of the problems we're discussing, men can be either blinded or belligerent about them. Some men are genuinely surprised to be told they have a problem with anger. They have been blind to the situation, and once their eyes are opened, they can set about changing it. Yet others are well aware of their temper. They figure, "That's the way I am. You just have to live with it." Many men seem to live with a chip on the shoulder. The belligerent man is, of course, much tougher to deal with. Such a person will probably require professional counseling if he'll go.

Although Jack seemed belligerent at first, he was actually a blinded man. In our first session, he wasn't convinced that anger was a problem for him. But when he came back for his second session, we went over his anger self-test. He scored high in anger, trust, and violence potential. "Wow!" he said. "I didn't think I was *that* angry."

Jack began to attend my group meetings. Group members, over the course of months, gave Jack valuable feedback on his behavior. Through them, he was able to see how angry he had been acting. In essence, the group held a mirror up to Jack, showing him the extent of his problem. And he began to make progress. After five months, he was no longer denying his anger, and he was not blaming others as much. He was learning healthier ways of expressing the energy within him. He was even gaining insight about how his upbringing was affecting his current attitudes.

"I still think that kids need strict parents, but I do know now that it's wrong to strike a child in anger," he said. "I hope my son doesn't have to be in some group twenty years from now talking about how he's all messed up because his father beat him. But now I don't think that's going to happen."

Chapter Eleven

The Passive Man

Gary has been chronically unemployed. He finally talked his wife, Jill, into supporting him while he went back to school to be trained for a professional career. During this time, he started drinking. Not a lot, but enough to make him lethargic most of the day.

His lack of work and lack of help around the house created a great chasm between Gary and Jill.

Then Gary and Jill had a child, and Gary had to quit school for a while to work full time. They had three children within five years. But as soon as the children were in school, Jill went back to work so that Gary could go back to school. He finally finished a bachelor's degree but was unable to find a suitable job. Today he works from time to time, but his wife is the major breadwinner. She also takes primary responsibility for the children and the house. She resents Gary's laziness immensely, and she flairs up at him regularly.

Gary is emotionally shut down, and several times a week, he drinks too much. He claims he is looking for the right job, but he does little to improve his situation. His self-image is shattered—he takes few risks and offers little emotional or verbal support to others. He has virtually no emotional interaction with his wife or kids. He might be considered clinically depressed, but he makes no effort to get help. His wife has given up trying to help him or change him, but she regularly threatens to leave him. I expect that one day she will.

Richard is also a passive man but in a different way. He goes to work each day with the consistency of a German railroad, departing each day at 6:00 A.M. and returning home at 7:00 P.M. His middle-management job is stressful. Richard works hard to meet quotas or at least to keep his boss off his back.

When he does get home, Richard is emotionally drained and has no energy left for his family. His wife's "job" is to keep the kids quiet and away from him. Maria knows that if she wants to keep peace in the house, he must not be disturbed. Weekends are not much better. That is Richard's time to recoup from the week. He might do a little work in the yard, but for the most part he watches sporting events on TV.

He feels he has a close relationship with Maria, but it's not really two-way. He will listen to her and empathize with her when he has the energy for it, but he doesn't share much about himself. He can talk about his boss, his job, the game he just watched, or how tired he is, but that's about the extent of his repertoire. True intimacy is difficult for Richard.

Unlike many passive men, Jose is quite successful in business. This is mostly due to some lucky breaks—such as inheriting his father's business. He is laid-back and easygoing, but he is married to a dynamo. His wife, Julie, is a sales rep.

Since Jose took over his father's business, he has kept it

running with competent employees—but he'd trade all of it for a shack on a beach in Hawaii. His wife, on the other hand, is constantly talking about building up the business, investing in expansion, and buying new houses or cars.

They have a fairly good marriage, as good as any I know, but no one would consider it traditional. Many would say that Jose's wife is the head of the family, and Jose might agree. He is quite content that way. Jose claims he has more that he could ever want or need in this world. He looks forward to early retirement and a condo at the beach.

We see three different types of passivity in these examples. Jose is passive at his job and generally in life. That's not necessarily a problem. He and his wife have different energy levels, different styles of living, perhaps different goals, and they will have to work through these issues. Still, Jose's passivity by itself is not a threat to their relationship. He does not love too little. In his communication with his wife, he is not passive at all.

Richard is the opposite. At work he is not passive, but at home he is. He gets the job done each day, but at home he shuts down emotionally. He is inaccessible to his family.

Gary is a combination. His passivity affects both his working life (what there is of it) and his home life. He never quite gets around to doing what he has to do. He has sunk within himself and sulks there, without meaningful interaction with his wife and children.

It is not wrong to be passive. Some men are naturally that way. But it can be a problem in a relationship if a man has become passive to avoid pain or intimacy.

But many women have a frustration that's much more serious: "I just can't get him to respond to me. I *wish* he'd get angry. Any response would do. But instead, all I get is silence or, at best, a few grunts and groans. How can I continue a relationship like this?"

ORIGINS OF PASSIVITY

Passivity can be a personality trait, inherited genetically from parents, just like brown hair or blue eyes. It may have some chemical basis, such as a lower level of testosterone. Some people are just born more passive.

It can also be a learned behavior. If a man's parents were passive (especially his father), he may learn to be passive. Parents are, of course, models—and many boys model themselves on their dads. We gain our arsenal of acceptable responses from our folks. If they are passive with each other and with life in general, a child will learn passivity.

Yet for others, passivity is a chosen strategy. That is, as boys encounter difficulties in dealing with their emotions, they may choose to shut down their emotions.

Children get hurt emotionally, more than we realize. And remember that boys, in general, are less equipped to cope with their emotions. Culturally and biologically, they are in a quandary about expressing their pains and working through them.

In a desperate attempt to regain control of their swirling emotions, many boys decide not to feel. This then becomes a pattern for their lives. In adulthood, nothing really matters to them.

CHARACTERISTICS OF THE PASSIVE MAN

How do passive men display their passivity? How can you tell if your man is a passive man? The following characteristics apply to many, though not all, passive men.

Introverted

The passive man tends to have a more introverted personality. Contrary to some people's expectations, an introvert can be social and friendly, but it takes work for him to be that way. The question is: Where does he find his energy? As a group, men tend to find their energy in solitude and expend it in social situations, while women do the opposite. John Gray talks of the cave into which men go, removing themselves from others to work on solving their problems. Passive men are even more that way. They tend to go deeper into the cave and stay there longer.

Of course, this trait of passive men can be terribly frustrating for the women who love them, especially if the women are extroverts. The women feel neglected.

Conflict Avoiding

Most passive men are conflict avoiders. They may have grown up in a chaotic home or have a low tolerance for turmoil. They quickly disengage whenever the conversation becomes too threatening. Conflict-avoiding behaviors can lead the passive man to avoid giving information that he is afraid will only create trouble. In other words, he tells you what you want to hear. He may even lie to you to keep peace.

Conflict avoidance seems rather benign until it interferes with a relationship. In a marriage, conflict avoidance is an impediment to a deepening relationship. Both partners need to express their needs and desires, and there will be occasional conflicts.

Pressure Avoiding

Passive men long for a stress-free life. They avoid any pressure, turn from responsibilities, and stay neutral on issues to keep from making decisions. They avoid promotions, self-destruct at jobs and in relationships, and avoid debates on controversial issues. As we saw with the examples that began this chapter, men can be active at work and passive at home or vice versa. Even if a man has a pressure-filled job, he may not know how to handle the pressure of an intimate relationship.

Emotionally Distant

It may seem that the passive man is hiding his true feelings from you. If so, he's also hiding his feelings from himself. He may not feel strongly about anything, or he may have developed a habit of burying his emotions so deeply that he can't show them. In any case, he seems emotionally distant. You want to make him happy, but you never know when he's happy.

Pouting or Sulking

A passive man might agree with you to end an argument but then pout or sulk about it. This is close to passive-aggressive behavior—giving in but harboring a grudge. At least the sulker has identified his true feelings, which passive men don't always do.

Low Self-Image

This *may* be a characteristic of the passive man, but it's not always present. Some passive men like themselves very much—that's why they spend so much time with themselves. But others are essentially afraid to come out of their shells. This attitude may have been instilled by passive or distant fathers and developed by a culture that prizes ambition and drive in men. As a result, some men may be ashamed of their passivity, but that shame holds them back even more.

Depression

Sometimes men are passive because they've been disappointed by life. If you don't feel, you won't get hurt. If you never try, you never fail. That can lead to a rather gloomy outlook on life. Nothing matters. The passive state feeds this depression. The passive man continues to be at the mercy of the events swirling around him. Since he does little to affect the events, he has no control over them, so he gets more deeply disappointed and cynical. Without good relationships to draw him out of his passivity, he sinks into a hopeless lethargy.

Impaired Sex Life

Passive men learn to restrict their desires.

They have found deliverance from difficult situations by removing themselves—emotionally or physically. They have found a certain peace in the absence of desire.

Sex is an engagement, an involvement. It also arises from a natural desire. If that desire has been watered down, and emotional connection is frightening, sex can be hard work. Your husband may do it to please you, to do his husbandly duty, but his heart and mind are miles away.

Addiction

Addiction may be an issue for some passive men. Passivity can arise from the same childhood wounds that can make a man ripe for addiction. Just like addiction, passivity is an escape, an escape from emotional involvement with the world around him. Addiction takes a basic desire and beats it to death. That's what the passive man is looking for, the deadening of desire.

Role Reversals

The wife of the passive man, out of necessity, may have become the more decisive, aggressive one in the relationship. In some cases, this role reversal occurs with minimal conflict. Often an aggressive woman will seek a relationship with a more passive man, so they will complement each other. But in other cases, the wife resists this role. She wishes her husband would play a more active role in the family, but after a while she gives up. She may even feel guilty about taking a leadership role in the family, but she learns that if she wants something done, she has to do it herself.

Difficult Transitions

It may take the passive man some time to summon the energy to move—or you may have to supply it. This applies not only to the couch potato but also to the man who's stuck at a certain level in a relationship. An emotional move takes extra energy, too.

The passive man may have a difficult transition from work to home—you want him to pop the noodles in the microwave and he's still noodling his last project at work. He may need an hour or more to unwind, vent, or be left alone. Transitions will also be difficult with the loss of a loved one or a move to a new home. In the meantime he may be quietly moody and frustrated.

UNDERSTANDING THE PASSIVE MAN

Why is your man passive? The answer may help you gauge your strategy.

Nature or Nurture

Look at his family, especially his father. Is a passive gene running around there? Or did he model his passivity on what he saw in his family growing up? If so, he comes by it naturally. He never learned how *not* to be passive. You may be able to nudge him out of it a bit, or you may have to learn to live with it.

Response to an Old Wound

Was he passive as a child? Or did he shut down his emotions in response to a particular trauma? The trauma may be something that in hindsight seems trivial—say, being picked on in fifth grade or jilted in junior high. But many boys decide to gain mastery in those moments by not feeling the pain. If the wound is major—sexual or physical abuse, for example—your man should see a counselor to work through the issues. But if it was a fairly mild problem, you can talk through it yourselves.

Overload

If your man is overworked at the job, he may shut down when he's with you. If he is with people all day long, he may need time alone. If a million extracurricular activities take up his time, he may have trouble focusing on you, so he may give up. If these things are true, both of you may need to evaluate your priorities.

Response to the Current Relationship

It's possible that your man is shutting down because of you. Are you an emotional (or physical) dynamo, operating at a pace far beyond his so that he can't keep up? He may stop trying.

Is he bored, pressured, or disappointed by your relationship? Many men expect marriage to maintain the magic of the first date or the honeymoon. Of course it doesn't. Marriage is hard work, and men may feel betrayed by that. Sometimes, then, men feel guilty for losing that initial spark. They may continue to go through the motions, but their emotions are swirling and they don't know how to verbalize them. So they shut down.

COPING WITH THE PASSIVE MAN

Depending on the reasons for your man's passivity, you may have different ways of coping. Here are some ideas.

Give Him Cave Time

He may need time to himself to collect his thoughts or recharge his batteries. It may be, say, a one-hour transition time when he gets home from work, or it may be a Saturday or Sunday afternoon. You may need to negotiate a certain amount of guilt-free time alone, but then draw him out and into family life.

Show an Interest in His Life but Don't Invade It

Never belittle his hobbies or sports. If he allows you to participate with him, use the valuable time together. But if he wants to reserve that as his own province, respect his wishes.

Give Him Small Tasks

If he feels overwhelmed, he may shut down. Praise whatever he did as a big help. He will gain a sense of accomplishment and be energized for your next request. If the task does not go well, don't berate him.

Praise Him in Public

Be careful about public teasing or criticism. It is hard enough for men to deal with social situations, and much more so when they feel that they're under attack. A man wants to feel admired and appreciated,[1] and a great way to make that happen is to show others how much he means to you. Men can shut down when they feel unimportant. If he feels nothing he does matters, he will do nothing. If he can't do anything right, why do anything at all? You need to show him how important he is to you.

Let Him Know What You Need from Him

This point functions on two levels—practical and personal. Practically, if things need to be done around the house, work together on a reasonable job list. Problems arise if he feels that you expect him to mow the lawn and paint the house and tune up the car all in one afternoon. He feels pressure, and he may shut down. Talk about it, and plan together.

But personally, you need to let him know what you need from him. Don't expect him to read your mind.

Live Your Own Life

John Gray offers several pointers on how to support a man in his cave, for example: "Don't sit next to the door of the cave and wait for him to come out. . . . Don't worry about him or feel sorry for him. . . . Do something that makes you happy."[2]

Don't be held back by your passive mate. Do the activities that you want to do. If he wants to join you, great. But if you need to go out alone, so be it.

Don't Feel Guilty About Filling a Leadership Vacuum

Some women assume that men should do certain things in the home—write the checks, discipline the kids, do the heavy lifting. But they have a hard time getting their men to do these things, so they do them—and then they feel guilty about it. Guilt leads to resentment. Resentment often makes the man shut down even more.

In such cases, you have basically two choices: (1) leave the tasks undone in the hopes that he will do them; (2) do them yourself. The first option seldom works.

NUDGING THE PASSIVE MAN

Don't expect great changes. You will not make your passive man an active man. But maybe you can nudge him into certain behaviors that will make your relationship run more smoothly.

Communication

Talk about your different styles. Talk about the origins of your man's shutdown. Allow for absolute honesty. Don't assume that you are the problem, but don't assume you're not. Don't overreact if he says something that wounds you. Get it out and talk through it.

Timing

Work with personal cycles. Learn about the times when he needs to be alone. Choose other times to talk. Tell him about the times when you need him to be with you. Ask him to give up some cave time to hold you.

Also, understand that it takes him longer to process his emotions, especially if he has shut them down. You must be patient with his attempts to open up to you. Don't rush him. Let him talk in his own timing.

Affirmation

Let your man know that his feelings are all right. Affirm his expressions of emotions, even if you may not understand them or appreciate them. Affirm the fact that he is expressing himself.

Somewhere along the line, your man learned that it was not okay to feel emotional or to express his emotions. You need to show him otherwise, day after day, week after week. Affirm him regularly, and in time he will get the message.

Drawing Out

But what if he never expresses emotion? You may still be able to find ways to draw him out. Ask gentle questions: "How was your day? What projects are you working on? Which is your favorite? What do you like about it?" Don't criticize his responses, and don't interrogate him. Accept what he gives you, but gently move to the next emotional level until he shuts down on you. Find things that he is emotional about, perhaps a hobby or sports team. Talk about his feelings for these things.

Boundaries

If he says, "I don't want to talk about it," that's it. Start again tomorrow. Always respect his boundaries. Do not invade his territory. He must open the border crossing to let you in. You must prove that you will do no damage once he lets you into his space.

Chapter Twelve

The Passive-Aggressive Man

Dave and Cindy were a match made in heaven. He was the Nordic weight lifter, she the model. They'd been dating for over a year, and everyone said they looked perfect together. The only problem was that Cindy was often extremely frustrated with Dave.

"He's constantly sending me double messages," she explained. "He'll say he's looking forward to coming over tonight, and then he'll show up two hours late. He buys me an expensive gift and then ignores me the rest of the evening. He tells me he'll take care of changing my oil but then never gets around to doing it. He tells me I'm beautiful but then gives me signals that he's embarrassed to be seen with me.

"So what's the story? Does he love me, or doesn't he? I feel so insecure about our relationship."

Cindy's description of Dave's behavior is a common complaint that I hear from clients about their fathers, husbands, and boyfriends. They are troubled by the inconsistency. One moment everything is going well, but in the next, it all falls apart. One day a man seems to be as loving and considerate as he can be, but then he turns stone-cold or, in some cases, vicious.

Is this a Jekyll-and-Hyde thing? No. We call the behavior passive-aggressive because it vacillates between these two extremes—passively accepting everything that comes along, then aggressively seeking revenge. The syndrome is common among men, and we often see it in their relationships with women.

When something happens that he doesn't like, the passive part of the passive-aggressive man will lead him down the path of least resistance: "No problem. Doesn't matter. Go with the flow." But while the purely passive man would shut down any negative response, the passive-aggressive man files it away. At some later time, the negative response comes out.

When Dave was late for his dates with Cindy, he was not trying to be mean to her. He was probably getting even subconsciously for something she had done to him the week before. Or maybe he didn't like being tied down, but he didn't want to tell her that directly.

This subconscious element makes passive-aggression difficult to figure out. If we fought all our fights immediately and openly, we would always know what we were fighting about. But passive-aggression is like a gopher you chase underground—who knows where or when it will surface again? When the aggression does surface, what is it responding to? Which "crime" is it seeking to punish?

ORIGINS OF PASSIVE-AGGRESSION

The term *passive-aggressive* was first used during World War II by an army psychiatrist, Dr. Menninger.[1] The behavior certainly existed before the war, but he was the first to name it and theorize its origins. He was studying soldiers who had strong negative reactions to military life. Due to the high degree of structure and control in the military, they learned (or knew instinctively) that fighting the system was fruitless. Therefore, they learned to express their displeasure with the military in other ways:

"Go along with it all but resist."

"I'll tell them I want to be here but make big mistakes so they'll transfer me or discharge me."

Corporal Klinger from the "M*A*S*H" TV series would be a good example. He begged repeatedly for a discharge from the army but found his protests only strengthened the system's determination to keep him in. The next time we see him he's the model soldier, saluting sharply with an enthusiastic attitude. Except for one thing—he's wearing women's clothing.

Organizations that foster similar authoritarian, highly structured environments are breeding grounds for the passive-aggressive person. They offer few avenues for individual expression and personal empowerment. Therefore, the person learns to get what he or she wants through other avenues—resistance, insubordination, indirect communication, and covert manipulation.

Families are the same way. When there is little opportunity for questioning, expression of needs, or a sense of empowerment, family members learn subtle ways to get what they want. They learn to pacify the authority (tell them what they want to hear) and then do what they want to do anyway. My mother used to call it sneaky. My wife calls it passive-aggressive.

Both men and women use this tactic, but there may be some slight differences in the way most men and women use passive-aggression. Women, I believe, are more likely to be passive-dependent—"I manipulate you by acting helpless, so I get you to do what I want"—while men are probably more aggressive in their manipulation. For example, if one wants someone else to pay a lunch bill, a woman might sit there with a blank look on her face while she waits for the man to pick up the check. But a man is more likely to say, "Whoops, I forgot my wallet" (even if he didn't).

Scott Wetzler, in his book *Living with the Passive-Aggressive Man*, notes that

> men are passive-aggressive in especially destructive and clumsy ways, upsetting or ruining love and world relationships—or world order. They torment themselves and you. For whatever reason—perhaps because women are socialized differently, learning charm and diplomacy at an early age, or because women have less testosterone—passive-aggression does not represent as serious a psychological problem or conflict for women as it does for men today.[2]

CHARACTERISTICS OF THE PASSIVE-AGGRESSIVE MAN

The passive-aggressive man acts and reacts in a number of typical ways. You may recognize some of these in your man's behavior. In truth, we may all use these techniques from time to time, but once again the key is whether or not this is the primary method of functioning in the relationship.

Conflicting Messages

The passive-aggressive man gives you mixed signals. He'll say, "I really want to be with you," while he explains why he has to go away for the next three weekends. If you're buying, say, a new car, he'll say, "Let's get the one *you* want," but he'll be sure to let you know which one *he* wants to buy, and he'll give you the silent treatment if you dare not comply.

This description makes him sound like a cad, a liar, a user—but the passive-aggressive man usually does not realize what he's doing.

Conflict Avoidance

This is the passive side of the passive-aggressive man. To avoid conflict, he'll avoid issues, he won't tell you the truth, or he'll mask his feelings. He gives the appearance that all is well when he's seething under the surface. He might use humor, charm, or generosity to be the life of the party, but he's hiding a much more cynical nature. He might act hurt, or weak, or seem to conform, when in truth he's manipulating you into following his agenda.

The passive-aggressive man usually does not know how to have a good argument. He is under the false impression that it is better to maintain a peaceful facade than to communicate difficult feelings. He may fear the pain of conflict or the results of his anger, or he may have a hard time communicating his true feelings.

Underlying Anger

The aggressive side of the passive-aggressive man is his underlying anger. Although he keeps an outward front of calm acceptance, he inwardly registers every time he thinks he's been cheated, every moment that he resents not being in control of a situation, every case where his desires have been ignored.

Your man will seldom show you the anger he feels toward you, but in your presence he may lash out at someone else. And you'll say, "Where did that come from?" You'll be surprised at the fury he expresses, as if the lid has been lifted from a boiling pot.

Many passive-aggressive men are afraid of their anger or can't verbalize why they are angry. They value self-control and may deny their anger, but it is obvious to anyone who gets close to them.

Indirect Communication

One person told me, "The only way I know how my father feels about me is to ask one of my brothers or sisters." Indirect communication is another way the passive-aggressive man will try to let you know of his anger or displeasure. It can be deliberate or unconscious.

At work, the passive-aggressive man might tell everyone how angry he is with his wife, but then tell her that all is well. Or perhaps he'll vent his frustrations to a mutual friend in the hope that his wife will eventually hear about it.

Avoidance of Intimacy

The passive-aggressive man is often cautious and guarded with his emotions. He is sensitive about being controlled or dominated, so he is hesitant to show vulnerability, weakness, or intimacy. He may allow his love to go only so far before he puts up obstacles or barriers. A single man might never allow the relationship to progress to a commitment level. Or a married man might create conflicts every time the relationship gets too close.

Putting You on the Defensive

One common characteristic of the passive-aggressive man is his ability to place the burden of blame on you. Many clients have come to see me because they are convinced that they're at fault or causing their husbands to react badly: "Is it me? I just don't get it." It may be partly you, but the passive-aggressive man would tend to make you feel that it is all you. Yes, you may contribute to the problem, but he must accept his responsibility in his reaction and behavior.

Deflected blame is a common tactic of the passive-aggressive man. When you do confront him on something, he will usually turn the tables back on you: "Why are you an hour late?" turns into "Why are you so impatient?"

Rationalization and Lying

The passive-aggressive man usually needs to come up with excuses to cover his lateness, incomplete projects, and sabotage. Sooner or later he begins to lie to you and then rationalize it because he doesn't want to upset you. He may tell you just enough so that he feels justified but withhold some critical details to keep you in the dark. The lies are probably minor, but if a passive-aggressive man gets in too deep, such as having an affair, he may say whatever he has to say to keep the peace.

Procrastination and Lateness

It is extremely frustrating to be in a relationship with a passive-aggressive man, or so I hear. Jesus told a parable about a father who told his two sons to go and work in the field. One said, "Sure, I'll go," but then he didn't. That was the passive-aggressive one. (The other said he wouldn't but did.) A passive-aggressive man will agree to do almost anything, but then he may put it off or be late with it.

Confrontation is uncomfortable. When you ask why the task is not accomplished, he must unleash a new set of promises or concoct false excuses: "I'm sorry, but something came up." Or "I got a flat on the way here." The passive-aggressive man insists on being overly nice to your face, which forces him to be overly inconsiderate later on.

IS IT MY FAULT?

Anyone who has been in relationship with a passive-aggressive person knows the emotional roller coaster you ride from self-doubt and blame to anger and indignation. You frequently feel that it's all your fault, but you don't know what you can change. And all of your attempts to change him don't seem to be doing any good.

Often women are attracted to passive-aggression in men, and they subtly encourage it. On the surface, passive-aggressive men can be charming, generous, and eager to please. By definition, they avoid conflict. So it may seem that you have found the perfect man with whom you can have a peaceful, pleasing relationship. But turbulent waters surge below.

When you see that turbulence, you may be tempted to ignore it or suppress it. But in so doing, you would be encouraging the pattern of passive-aggression.

The passive-aggressive man is more likely to flourish in relationship with one of the following personality types: the child, the parent, or the missionary.

The Child

"The child" has a dependent personality. Because this person tends to be more passive and less likely to confront, she enjoys the passive side of the passive-aggressive man, and she puts up with the aggressive side. Because of her lack of confrontation, she allows the passive-aggressive man to continue being late, to keep on lying, and to maintain a double life. In addition, many wives or girlfriends in the child role believe that they don't deserve any better, and they are more likely to accept blame.

The Parent

"The parent" tries to manage the life of the passive-aggressive man. He may be a very competent, mature man, but the wife assumes the parental role. Perhaps she lays out his clothes or at least critiques what he wears. Or she monitors his cholesterol intake over breakfast and sends him off to work.

The passive-aggressive man will not confront you with the way he really feels. If he resents your control, he will not say so, but he will find other ways to assert his independence. One man told me about his wife's efforts to monitor his calorie intake: "She would make me a special low-fat breakfast, so I'd stop on the way to work and pick up a dozen creme donuts."

The Missionary

This type of woman has a "holier than thou" attitude. 'The missionary" is always telling the man in her life to shape up, change his ways, or get right with God. She urges him to pray more, pressures him to quit drinking, or drags him to church events. This may sound like the parent again, but with the missionary, control is not the issue as much as moral or political courage. In both cases, the woman has the perceived upper hand; therefore, the man feels threatened. Rather than confront her, he goes along verbally, but his behavior subverts the words.

Understand this man's double bind. For example, he may genuinely want a relationship with God, but his wife is pushing him into *her* relationship with God. If he opposes her directly, he's going against God—at least it feels that way. So he lets her impose the forms of faithfulness on him, but he resists inwardly.

UNDERSTANDING THE PASSIVE-AGGRESSIVE MAN

Men are always keeping score. We weigh everything that happens and add an appropriate number of points to the score. The passive-aggressive man keeps a careful tally (but usually an inflated tally) of what he is owed. If he feels that the score is lopsided against him (and he almost always feels that way), he will find a way to even the score. As we have said, this "evening" may occur through an explosion of anger but regularly happens in subtler ways—bad attitude, secret sabotage, private indiscretions.

You might say the motto of the passive-aggressive man is: "I don't get mad; I get even!"

COPING WITH THE PASSIVE-AGGRESSIVE MAN

Living with a passive-aggressive man can be a challenge. If he insists on acting in a passive-aggressive manner, there's not a lot you can do to change him. But you can try to create a better environment and lessen the effects of his passive-aggression.

Be Honest

If you are joining your man in hiding your true feelings, you're reinforcing his behavior. Tell him how you really feel, positively or negatively. Make it a point to sit down with him every so often for a reality check. He may hate this, but you need to do it so that both know what the score is.

Welcome Healthy Conflict

Learn how to disagree respectfully. Don't let him back down from a conflict, even if that means you have to help him argue his side. Of course, healthy conflict does not include name-calling, blaming, and violence.

Find Creative Compromises

Both of you may want to win all the time, but you can't. Discover ways to meet in the middle to keep both of you satisfied.

Be Wise to His Tricks

If you sense passive-aggressive behavior in your man, be aware that he may lie to you. You don't need to accuse him regularly, but you do want to bring his dissatisfaction out into the open.

Don't Play the Blame Game

If any conflict comes out into the open, he will probably blame you. You should always be willing to share blame if he will share it with you, but don't accept it all.

Find Supportive Friends

A passive-aggressive man can play tricks with your mind. You need regular reality checks with trusted friends or mentors. They can help you evaluate your opinions of what's going on in your relationship with your man. You don't want them to negotiate the issues of your marriage, but they can help you keep things in perspective.

See a Counselor

If you suspect there's a problem with passive-aggression, try to see a professional counselor together. Your man may resist, but he will probably go along with it to keep peace (and, of course, make you pay later). Often a counselor can help dig up a man's inner feelings.

NUDGING THE PASSIVE-AGGRESSIVE MAN

Your first step in changing the unhealthy patterns in your relationship might be difficult and painful for you. You must first look at yourself and your tendency to be a child, a parent, or a missionary. This self-examination might require the help of a close friend or even the man you are trying to nudge. You might ask him to read the descriptions of the three types and comment on any that resemble you. Then graciously accept his answer without defending yourself. Attacking him now will only increase his passive-aggressive behavior.

This is only a first step. I am not saying that you bear all the blame for your situation, but you may be contributing unwittingly to the negative patterns. Your purpose is to establish an adult-adult relationship. You don't want to parent him or let him parent you. Learn to talk together as equals.

The next step is to allow him to individualize. Give him some independence. Let him be the unique individual he is. Let him be responsible for his own life and choices (and you for yours).

Next, find ways to empower him to make his own choices and to live with the consequences. Stop rescuing him from the results of his mistakes or allowing him to continue his double life. Control and self-determination are core issues in the development of passive-aggressive tendencies. If the man in your life is feeling controlled, he must feel more empowered. His perceptions might be totally distorted, but that is still the way he feels. Find ways of changing that feeling. Let him know all his choices. For instance, instead of giving him a list of chores on Saturday, discuss with him the plans he has or the projects he would like to get done. If you do need some work done, present it with optional times and a flexible schedule, and maybe even some names and estimates of what it would cost to have someone else do it. (The thought of saving some money might motivate him even more.)

Talk, talk, talk, and listen. Silence is the breeding ground for passive-aggression. Honest conversation can be the cure. You need to take the lead in talking about your relationship, and you need to ask the hard questions. But—this is very important—you must not overreact when your hard-to-ask questions are met with hard-to-hear answers.

One of the issues you must bring out into the open is blame. You have to talk about who's to blame. If you don't address this directly, your man's scoring system will run wild against you. The fact is that many men (and many women) are dissatisfied with certain aspects of their lives. He can easily start to blame you for everything he's dissatisfied with.

You have to talk about dissatisfaction and its causes. What have you *both* gained and given up in the relationship? How have you helped each other? Make sure he gives you the plus points as well as the minus. Make sure he sees your side, too.

A final nudging point: Let him know how much you appreciate him. Major penalty points get tacked on when he thinks you don't appreciate all that he does for you. Yes, there is a double standard here. He probably does not let you know how much he appreciates all you do for him, and he should. He probably doesn't realize all you do for him. As a female friend of mine quipped, "When I take out the trash, it's my job. When he does it, it's a favor." You may need to make the passive-aggressive man feel successful even when there is little to praise.

Chapter Thirteen

The Compulsive Man

Ralph was a factory worker who didn't like his life very much. He'd come home from work, go to the fridge and grab a beer, then sit and watch TV until bedtime. His wife, Chloe, was frustrated with his lethargy, but he justified it by saying how hard his job was. In time, Chloe took over most of the responsibilities in the home, including paying bills, doing housework and yard work, and even making minor repairs. She regularly complained to Ralph that he should be helping her, but he turned her off and turned up the volume on the TV. He seemed to shut down all his feelings toward her; their love life was nonexistent. He had a better relationship with the refrigerator than with her.

Chloe's criticism caused Ralph to feel worse and worse about himself. He *was* tired, but he was also lazy.

By the time Ralph came to see me for counseling, he was depressed, out of work, and about to lose his wife to another man. I was alarmed by the pattern of his drinking. Alcohol was an escape for him. He relied on it to save him from his other problems. I asked him about it, but he insisted that he could handle it. "I never drive drunk," he protested. "I only drink at home. My wife's nagging forces me to do it. Drinking's not my problem."

"Fine," I said. "Then why don't you stop drinking for a while so we can deal with these other things—your marriage, your job, your depression."

He couldn't do that. Again and again I urged him to seek treatment for his alcoholism, but he denied that he had a problem. Finally, I gave up. There was nothing I could do.

A few years later, I happened to see Ralph. He was a changed man. He said that his family had gotten together and confronted him about his alcoholism. He finally had to face it. "You were right all along, Doc," he told me. "Sorry I didn't listen."

Ralph had recognized his problem and sought treatment for it. His life and marriage had totally turned around.

WHAT IS COMPULSION?

Compulsive-addictive behavior comes in many forms. Many men are addicted to alcohol or drugs or cigarettes, some to food. Some men are workaholics while others seem to be addicted to exercise. Gambling addiction is common, and for some men, their overattention to sports can be close to a compulsion. We find sex addiction in a large number of men. Relationship addiction is less common in men than in women, but it does exist. We might even say that some men are addicted to anger or control (though we deal with those issues in more depth in other chapters). The testimony of men who routinely abuse their wives or girlfriends indicates that some compulsion may be at work there.

Note that we are dealing with many different types of problems—from substance abuse to compulsive behavior. There is also a wide range of seriousness involved, with different strategies to overcome the problems. Obviously, the addictions to alcohol, illegal drugs, and nicotine have a chemical component. But case workers have found that you can get a man off heroin chemically, and he is likely to go right back to it unless he deals with the inner compulsion.

This is probably the most difficult set of problems we'll deal with in this book, and I don't promise to have all the answers—especially for the more serious compulsions. But you may find some shreds of wisdom here if you are living with a compulsive-addicted man.

Where do they come from, these drives that ruin men and their relationships? Picasso once said that art was "a lie that speaks the truth." You might say the same thing about compulsive behavior.

Most men are living a lie. Women help them do it.

There are wounds deep in the souls of many men, wounds that have festered because they have gone untreated. Men do not bring their pain out into the open as easily as women do. And our society, male and female, has collectively rewarded men for covering up their insecurities, for keeping their private wounds private.

Most researchers agree that compulsive-addictive behavior stems from some root pain or shame. These are often childhood issues that have been covered over but have not been adequately dealt with. As my colleague Vincent Gallagher writes, "Ignoring or suppressing emotions only increases their ability to affect us. In counseling circles there is a saying: 'What you don't deal with deals with you.' In other words, internalized pain is the fuel that fires the flames of compulsive behavior."[1]

The pains that prompt compulsive behavior may be long forgotten or even blocked out by the mind, but they long to come out. The man who suffers from these pains has a problem. He is locked into a lifestyle that won't let him own up to these ancient wounds (and he may not even know what they are). But the pains have to come out somehow. They often force a man into unhealthy actions.

The various behaviors have various motives. But let me simplify things by saying that compulsive-addicted men are usually trying to escape, confess, punish themselves, or prove themselves.

Escape

Escape by itself is not a bad thing. We have all taken vacations to escape from the routine of life for a while. The problem occurs when the escape is unhealthy, uncontrolled, or overly distracting.

Drugs and alcohol are unhealthy escapes. They may provide a temporary escape from the awareness of your troubles, but they hurt your mind and body. You can say the same thing about working all the time.

Other escapes can be uncontrolled. Addictions often take over a person's life. Despite a person's attempts to manage the problem, the problem usually grows to unmanageable proportions. The sex addict starts cruising every night and losing sleep, which affects his work. The gambling addict taps into the mortgage money for one more "sure win."

Compulsive escapes can be distracting. The escapee loses his focus on the important things in life by drifting off into the fantasy world of his addictions.

The escapee is looking for this distraction. The primary lure of most addictions is that they're easy, at least to start. Even the workaholic may find that he is in his element on the job.

Confession and Self-Punishment

Many compulsive-addicted men have low self-esteem, but they tend to hide it. Addictions are a way of coming clean, of evening the score: "You may think I've got my life together, but I really don't—and here, I'll prove it to you." Almost a fear of success is at work. The better a man's life becomes, the more he realizes he doesn't deserve it. He fears that some ultimate force will bring him down anyway, so he does something to sabotage his success before he climbs too high.

For the compulsive-addicted man, maybe it's the male sense of justice, combined with self-doubt, that keeps reminding him that he doesn't deserve what he has. In many situations, it's not just self-doubt but shame. A man may feel guilty for some past misdeed and may insist on doing penance for it.

Proving Oneself

Other addictions arise as desperate attempts to climb out of poor self-esteem. They propel men forward along certain paths at breakneck speed. Workaholics are like this; so are some sex addicts and perhaps exercise maniacs or anorexics.

The inner monologue goes like this: "I am not good enough. If I accomplish this, I will be good enough." But when that thing is accomplished, the man still doesn't feel good enough, so he sets a new goal. The goal may be a certain project at work or a particular level of employment or income. For the sex addict, it may be the seduction of a particular woman, then another particular woman. Some bodybuilders set their sights on a particular weight or muscle mass or strength level, and even if they have to take dangerous steroids, they'll do it.

This type of compulsive-addicted man is often trying to make up for a childhood insecurity.

Many workaholics, too, are driven by a need to make something of themselves. Often they are trying to prove themselves to their fathers or to other authority figures. But even if that fantasy encounter does happen, and a man finally gets the approval he has sought, by then the behavior patterns are usually so deeply entrenched that the compulsive man is stuck. He must prove himself to many other people. Ultimately, he must prove himself *to himself*.

LIVING WITH A COMPULSIVE-ADDICTED MAN

"Addiction is a lie that speaks the truth." The truth, as I've said, is that many men are deeply wounded. Despite the masculine image they may present, there are serious hurts that can ooze out in various self-destructive compulsions.

But make no mistake about it: Addictions are lies. They promise escape but bring bondage. They promise fulfillment but yield frustration. Addiction changes a person's perception of what's normal. And that skews every action, every relationship.

If you are married to, or closely involved with, a compulsive-addicted man, his addiction is part of your life. You can't avoid it. Especially with that male ability to compartmentalize, he may feel that he can keep his problem hidden—but he can't. It will affect your relationship. It will affect you. You will need to take some bold, confrontative action if you want to make things better.

Understanding

You can maintain a healthy perspective if you keep these two thoughts in front of you: (1) Yes, your addicted man may be a victim, and (2) he still chooses to feed his addiction. Change is necessary on both fronts. By attempting to heal the ancient wounds, one can ease the pressure that pushes a man into his addiction. But the well-worn track of the addictive behavior must be repaved. That requires a man's conscious choice, a will to change.

As the addicted man seeks to change his behavior, your behavior may have to change, too. You will need to give a boost to his healthy efforts and stop conspiring with him to hide or manage the problem. More on that later.

Understand also the various ploys of the addicted man.

Denial/Repression

"What problem?" The addicted man usually refuses for a long time to admit to himself that he is addicted. It can take even longer to admit that to anyone else. Trust your perception. Your best action at this stage is to hold a mirror up to him. Let him know how his behavior has been changing. If he used to go out for a drink once a week and now it's every day, tell him so. Give him the facts of what he's doing, so it will be harder for him to deny his situation.

Rationalization

As the addicted man becomes aware of his addiction, he begins to make excuses. This is a "defensive maneuver," says Gerald G. May. "These rationalizations are not intentional lies; the person actually tries to convince [himself] that they are true."[2]

By rationalizing, a man is saying, "There are reasons for what I do. Therefore, my behavior is okay." In some way, he begins to view the behavior as necessary, considering his "special case." The problem is that this reasoning is half true. There are reasons behind addictions, as we have seen, yet that does not make the behavior okay. The man is responsible for his choices.

Watch out for the wild saber of blame, as the addicted man whirls it around him. He may begin to blame you for his problems, drawing you into the whole process of denial, rationalizing, hiding, and so on.

Hiding

The addicted man may get to the point where he knows he's addicted, but he doesn't want anyone else to know. This can be a time of deep depression, though the addict may become adept at hiding his true emotions. He will seek to hide his offending behavior from you, if possible, and he may seek your help in hiding the behavior from others.

Delaying Change

"I'll change on New Year's; I'll make a resolution." "I'm going through a tough time at work right now; when that's over, I'll change." "I have to give this more thought." He may seem sincere in his desire to change, but such statements are likely delaying tactics. "Someday" never comes.

Surrender

Sometimes addicted people can give up the struggle. They can resign themselves to their addiction. This can be a point of belligerence; they insist that you accept them and their addiction as well.

Management

An addicted person may try to manage the problem, keeping it under a certain control. This tactic gives the illusion that the problem is not a problem, and it restores a little self-respect. But the addicted man is fooling himself. Most addictions defy management. They may be controlled for a while, but they will soon grow again.

The fierce male independence will cause many men to park

at this level: "Leave me alone. I can handle it. I've got it covered." You may need to back off for a while, but don't accept the lie.

Coping

You will be tempted to go along with the denial, rationalization, or hiding. There can be many practical reasons for working with your man to hide his problems. If his addiction causes him to lose his job, for instance, that will hurt you as well. But ultimately, such collusion is harmful. The road to wholeness goes through confession and openness.

It is essential, once again, that you establish proper boundaries. Draw up clear guidelines about what behavior is acceptable and what is not: "If I find you doing drugs in this house again, I'm taking the kids and leaving." That's a good, clear boundary line—*if* you are willing to carry it out.

Let me repeat that I believe in marriage and I do not encourage wives to leave their husbands. But in extreme cases, separation may be necessary for the health of the people involved. Serious addictions can create dangerous situations for everyone involved.

You must accept the fact that your man will probably not reform without outside help. You may do everything right and still see the man you love sink down and down. It is painful and frustrating—but it's not your fault.

Nudging

Nudges seldom work with a compulsive-addicted man. Perhaps if your man is just beginning to slide into compulsive behavior, you might take subtle steps to halt that slide. But most of the addictions we're talking about are serious business. They require serious action.

You will not change his behavior, no matter how great your love or determination. *He must decide to change himself.*

Having said that, let me suggest some things you can do that might help.

Locate a Counselor

You might go with your man to counseling a few times, but ultimately, the compulsive man must decide to go by himself. Until the man decides he wants to get help, there's not much a counselor can do. But you can do the research, scout out a good therapist, and put the phone number in your man's hand. Be sure the counselor is familiar with treating addictions. And be prepared: Even your advance work may meet with some resistance. Your man may want to think it's his idea.

Arrange for Intervention

This group activity should be organized by a trained counselor. Addicts, as we've said, deny their problems and try to hide them. They often deceive family members and play one against the other to keep their charade going. An intervention is basically a meeting in which all the family members and/or close friends gather to confront the addict with his problem. No more lies. No more taking sides. We all want what's best for the addict. Done in love and honesty, this can be a powerful jolt to an addicted man.

Do Root Research

This can be tricky, but you might coach your man in digging out the root reasons for his addiction. This approach is especially helpful if he resists seeing a counselor.

Ask questions such as these:

- "How do you feel when you do this [the addictive behavior]?"

- "At what times do you feel most tempted?"
- "In what circumstances are you most tempted?"
- "When did you start doing this?"
- "What people do you think of when you do this?"
- "What do you think about yourself as you do this?"

These basic questions may open up some understandings.

Keep a Journal

As painful as it may be, note the incidents that occur in your man's addiction. How many times has he come home drunk? How many affairs has he had? How much money did he lose last week gambling? How many days has he missed from work? This objective record will keep you and him from denying the problem. The journal may force you to face facts.

Look for Substitute Addictions

It isn't the best approach, but sometimes it works. Recovering alcoholics often take up smoking. Smokers who quit may start to eat compulsively. Former overeaters may throw themselves into exercise. As long as the new master is kinder than the old one, it's probably a step in the right direction. The root issues are obviously still there, but they're being played out in less harmful ways.

Leave

If you are single and involved with an addicted man, my advice is straightforward: Get out. He will drag you down. Save yourself. If you are married to him, I believe you should do everything you can to uphold the marriage vows. But when things become dangerous for you and/or your children, consider a separation. His problems do not have to be your problems—especially if he resists all attempts to be healed.

Pray

God works miracles. He answers our prayers, but He seldom does exactly what we expect. But He has the power to change lives, the power to heal. If your man cries out for deliverance and cooperates with the deliverance process, God can deliver him. But will your man do that? As you wait and wonder, you may find yourself understanding more about God, who offers spiritual health to a world of people who refuse to take it. He grieves with you as your man spurns any attempt at wholeness. But He rejoices with you as He helps your man take those first baby steps of faith on the road to a life free of addictions.

Chapter Fourteen

The Supervisor, the Sponge, and the Stranger

We have talked about how men tend to be more self-centered than women. Thankfully, most men do not carry it to the extreme. But we can define several types of men who express their self-orientation in distinct, and sometimes extreme, ways.

The controlling man (the supervisor) dominates the lives of those around him. He has an exalted opinion of his wisdom, and he believes that all others are there to serve him.

The self-absorbed man (the sponge) does his own thing. He will not dominate, but he will neglect. He tends to have an exalted opinion of everything he does and considers everyone else (even a wife) unimportant.

The commitment-phobic man (the stranger) is afraid to commit himself to others in a meaningful relationship. He might have a high or low opinion of himself, but he is afraid to lose that self to someone else. His "I" is so strong, he can't contemplate a "we."

THE CONTROLLING MAN

Controlling men are not easy to spot. Don't expect leather jackets and gold chains. Often controlling men control by their charm. They seem gracious, giving, good listeners. Whether consciously or subconsciously, they know how to do their research. They scout out their avenues to control.

Why do so many men feel the need to control others?

One answer is ego. He may be so sure he is right that he doesn't trust anyone else to control things.

Another explanation might be perfectionism. The controlling man may have a strong vision of the way things should be. If you share his vision, you're fine; but if you don't, he must tell you what to do.

There's also tradition. For generations, men have been in control of most facets of life or at least thought they were. Many men today are following their fathers' examples. For them, that's what it means to be a man, to be king of your castle.

Some controlling men appeal to religious teaching. They believe that the scriptural appointment of the husband as head of the wife gives him complete lordship over the home. Now, I believe in the Bible, and I follow its teaching, but this male lordship is a distortion of what the Bible really says.

Anthropologists may cite the male pack mentality. Men often view things hierarchically—"I answer to him, and these people answer to me." Our military and many businesses—run by men—are set up that way. In such a system, you determine your worth by the scope of your control. How many departments, how many people, and how many operations are in your control? If you are low man on the totem pole, you're not worth much.

And some controlling men are blind.

Controlling men seem to be stuck in the early stages. They see only themselves, and they are convinced that the world revolves around them. They grab everything around them for their pleasure, to fulfill their needs. The controlling man is blind to your personhood. You exist for his pleasure.

Coping and Nudging

How do you handle a controlling man? Start by shoring up your self-esteem. A controller majors on the manipulation of others. He may try to destroy your self-image so that you will have to depend on him.

Author Judith Segal calls these men "Executives":

> Often, when Executives meet you, they love who you are. They say, "You're outgoing, you're assertive, and you're pretty. You make me laugh, and you're smart." Then, as the relationship progresses, they start to criticize the same qualities they loved you for in the beginning.[1]

That criticism can tear you apart: "What am I doing wrong? He used to like these things! Why don't I please him anymore?" Flattery has led you into the fold, but once you're penned in, you get fleeced.

To restore your self-esteem, stop believing the negatives he throws at you. If he picks on you all the time, shut it off.

You must develop or restore outside friendships. Friends will help you gain a perspective on your situation. They will bolster your self-esteem. But don't spend your whole time talking about your controlling man—talk about who you are. Your man will probably not like your outside friendships—that's okay. But to avoid misunderstanding, limit your closest friendships to other women.

Find an activity that's all yours. Do something that physi cally gets you out of his domain and gives you a personal emotional outlet. You need to show yourself and your man that you are a real person, even apart from him.

Just say no. If he makes an unreasonable request, refuse it. He may get angry, but you can take it. Choose your point of defiance wisely; don't fight World War III over an unimportant issue. Know where your major boundaries are, and cling to them.

Talk about it. It is not likely that a controlling man will give up his control because you ask him to, but he may not realize how controlling he is. It may be a pattern he learned in his upbringing, and he may not know any other way to be. Talk about your feelings. Let him know what you need from him. See if he will work together with you to build a marriage based on teamwork.

You might find models of noncontrolling behavior. Select other couples who have mutually respectful relationships and socialize with them. Let your man see that he does not need to build his self-respect on his domination of you.

If you are in a dating relationship with a controlling man, get out of it. Or insist on change, and leave if he refuses.

If you are married to a controlling man, you must do your best to live with him. But if he crosses the line, be ready to take action. Where's your line? I don't know. His behavior may become so severe that you must get away from him for your safety.

If at all possible, get counseling for your relationship. If your man is willing to listen, perhaps a counselor can give him some perspective and find a way for him to stop controlling you.

THE SELF-ABSORBED MAN

Greg is in love with himself. He's an actor, and he's sure he'll make it big someday. The only problem is that he can't sing, he's mediocre at acting, and he's only a fair dancer. But he doesn't realize any of that. He strides into auditions with confidence, and he's managed to snag some good roles in community theaters.

There's something attractive in confidence. And Greg has used it to go surprisingly far on his meager talent. People love a self-assured man. But Greg goes beyond that. He is self-absorbed. He is so wrapped up in his own needs and goals that he can't pay attention to anyone else's.

Self-absorbed men share many of the same traits as controllers, but they're less dangerous. A self-absorbed man will not dominate you; he'll use you or ignore you. He will probably frustrate you. You want to be part of his dream, but he won't let you in. You help him, and you expect some gratitude, but he has his own agenda to follow.

As I said, his world revolves around him. And in many cases he may have the energy and charisma that draw others into his orbit. He exerts a kind of gravity that may pull you in as well. There's nothing wrong with participating in his life, but life with a self-absorbed man tends to be greatly out of balance.

As I mentioned in chapter 9, an extreme level of self-absorption is narcissism. Here's how the *Diagnostic and Statistical Manual* defines the *narcissist*:

> A pervasive pattern of grandiosity (in fantasy or behavior), lack of empathy, and hypersensitivity to the evaluation of others . . . as indicated by at least five of the following:
>
> 1) Reacts to criticism with feelings of rage, shame, or humiliation (even if not expressed)
>
> 2) Is interpersonally exploitive: takes advantage of others to achieve his or her own ends
>
> 3) Has a grandiose sense of self-importance, e.g., exaggerates achievements and talents, expects to be noticed as "special" without appropriate achievement

4) Believes that his or her problems are unique and can be understood by only other special people

5) Is preoccupied with fantasies of unlimited success, power, brilliance, beauty, or ideal love

6) Has a sense of entitlement . . . e.g., assumes that he or she does not have to wait in line when others must do so

7) Requires constant attention and admiration

8) Lack of empathy: inability to recognize and experience how others feel . . .

9) Is preoccupied with feelings of envy[2]

These problems can occur in moderately self-absorbed men, but if this description fits your man to a T, you may be involved with a narcissist. If so, I urge you to get counseling as soon as you can.

At this level, the apparently high self-regard is masking a seriously damaged self-esteem. "The person may be pre-occupied with how well he or she is doing and how well he or she is regarded by others," states the *Diagnostic and Statistical Manual*, which also cites an "almost exhibitionistic need for constant attention and admiration." The manual adds, "The person may constantly fish for compliments, often with great charm. In response to criticism, he or she may react with rage, shame, or humiliation, but mask these feelings with an aura of cool indifference."[3]

I don't think all self-absorbed people are masking insecurity. At more moderate levels, I think many are just stuck on themselves. But when the outward actions are covering deep personality damage, as with the narcissist, professional help is required.

Coping and Nudging

It's possible to live with a self-absorbed man; you just have to keep reminding him you're there. If you are content to live independent, parallel lives, you'll be fine. But you're probably looking for a bit more intimacy.

First, you must deal with your rejection issues. Many women have wounds of rejection from the past. In many cases, a father or big brother regularly put them down or ignored them. Often the departure of a parent, through divorce or death, has made a woman feel rejected.

If you struggle with rejection, you may need a counselor's help. On your own, you can try to put your relationship in perspective. See each issue for what it is, and do not draw conclusions about your value.

Live your own life. Finding your own activities may have no effect on your man, but it will make you a stronger person. It may also pull you away from the gravitational pull he has on your life.

Provide close accountability. If your man is self-absorbed and merely blinded to it (rather than belligerent about it), he may give you permission to hold him accountable. I know many men (including myself) who could become much more self-centered if it weren't for wives who hold us closely accountable, insisting that we be more giving and sacrificial. Speak to your man frankly but lovingly whenever he becomes too self-focused.

Make sure your needs are met. I know a woman who works hard at her job and struggles to make ends meet for herself and her children. Meanwhile, her husband has a high-paying job and lives comfortably. No, they're not divorced; he's self-absorbed. He's a golf fanatic, spending big bucks on equipment and fees and outings, but he keeps his wife and the kids on a meager allowance. He won't buy health insurance for them because he thinks it's a rip-off.

Finally, the wife decided to keep her paycheck (she had been signing it over to him) and use it to care for the kids. She bought health insurance for herself and the children (but not him). Obviously, this is not the ideal home situation, but his extreme self-absorption forced her to take these measures.

You may have financial needs or emotional needs that must be met. If your husband will not help, find others who will. Of course, I am *not* advocating sexual infidelity, but you'll need to find supportive friendships outside the home.

Tell him what you need—in his terms. You have to tell your man when you need attention, when you need conversation, when you need a word. And you need to tell him in his language. Men's language is action oriented and self-oriented, but not feeling oriented.

Do not say, "I feel lonely," and expect him to do something about it. Say, "I need to go out on a date. Why don't you take me out to dinner tonight?" He can respond to the self-need and the point of action.

Do not try to edge into the corners of his consciousness and then sulk if he doesn't notice you and focus on you. If you want his full attention, you have to ask for it clearly.

Some will tell you to get involved in his activities, but your involvement is likely to be an intrusion. My "golf widow" friend tried to go golfing with her husband once. He couldn't handle it. He needed to be by himself (or with his golf buddies), and she felt rejected more than ever.

The good news is that many men are self-absorbed in a blinded way. He doesn't realize how narrow his scope is. He needs to grow up, to enlarge his vision, and you can help your man do this.

The bad news is that some men are belligerently self-absorbed. He is self-centered and proud of it. It's very difficult to get into the heart of a man like this.

THE COMMITMENT-PHOBIC MAN

In recent years, single men have been ribbed about avoiding the *c* word, that is, *commitment*. Of course, not all men are afraid of commitment, but a substantial number are. Most of them are, as you might guess, single. Some of them are rogues, looking to use women for sexual pleasure. But others are nice guys, who develop well-rounded relationships but can't pull that commitment trigger. The nice guys are more frustrating; at least you can recognize the rogues and put on your armor.

What's the Problem with Commitment?

Why are so many men afraid to get married? Why do so many avoid even going steady? What is so all-fired important about keeping options open?

The Myth of the Better Woman

Remember that men are always keeping score. We may pride ourselves on dating a nine, but what if a ten comes along? Our minds are filled with images from Hollywood and Madison Avenue of beautiful women. We are trained to fantasize about these women. Men need to keep options open in case one of these fantasies might come true.

The Ease of Shallow Relationships

Why bother to commit when my needs are met in a noncommittal relationship? Men don't have the depth of emotional needs that women have—or at least we're not as aware of those needs. Give us a date for Saturday night, and we're happy. In today's sexually liberated environment, shallow relationships aren't hard to find. And many men are satisfied with them.

The Lure of Variety

If relationships are only skin-deep, they can get boring rather quickly. One solution is to deepen the relationship, to actually commit, but that's too threatening. The other solution is to seek variety in dating life: "If this is Tuesday, this must be Felicia." Some men take a strange pride in how many girlfriends they have. They are following the playboy philosophy to the letter.

The Pain of the Past

Many men have been hurt in previous relationships. Remember that men do not process emotional pain as well as women do. We wall it off. And we build walls against ever loving again.

The Inflation of Self

This applies mostly to men who have been single for a long time. If you've had time to find yourself, if you're in that process, if you're building a career, or if you're used to living by yourself, the merger with another human being will be difficult. Sure, there's a lot to gain, but the unmarried man doesn't know that. He sees only that he will invariably lose some of his own self, which he has worked so hard to develop.

The February 1994 issue of *Christian Single* magazine asked readers to comment on men's fear of commitment. There were some interesting responses. A man from South Carolina agreed that men were afraid of commitment "because they'd have to give up too much of themselves. They don't want to let down their walls. Basically, men are a little bit selfish, especially if they have been single for a long time like me. We don't want to give up things that are comfortable."

The Definition of Love

Too many guys are waiting for the bolt from the blue, the lightning strike that will make them madly in love with that special woman. It doesn't always happen. When it does, it's often with the wrong woman.

I think many guys have bought some image of love from the movies. They're waiting for the screen to go fuzzy as they view her across a crowded room. They may wait a long time.

The One for My Life

There are schools of thought that a mate is chosen for everyone who's supposed to get married. As a teenager, I was taught to keep my eyes open because at any moment I might be shown the one for my life. Happily married couples regularly reported how they "just knew" they were the right ones for each other. I think this attitude—fear of a wrong commitment—may keep some men from committing themselves.

But it's ridiculous to live in fear that "the one" may have walked by you while you were tying your shoelace.

The Permanence of Marriage

This reason for commitment-phobia is the flip side of a good thing. A single man, a Christian, told me recently, "I think I wouldn't be so afraid of commitment if I believed in divorce. If divorce was okay, I might try out marriage to see if it worked. If not, no problem. But I believe that marriage should be forever, so I want to be very careful about making that commitment."

The Complicity of Women

This comment may be cynical, but I think men shy away from commitment because women let them. A woman will commit herself, emotionally or otherwise, to a man who won't commit himself. A woman will often seek to prove that she is marriage worthy by offering all the joys of marriage.

Commitment-phobia may also be found in marriage. If you happen to marry a commitment-phobic man, you may find that he remains aloofly independent and distant. He may not want to engage you on a deeper level due to his insecurity or fear of rejection: "If you find out what's deep inside me, you might reject me."

Coping and Nudging

If you are involved with a commitment-phobic man, you need to determine whether he is a terminal commitment-phobic or whether he's slow. If he is slow, you need to determine how long you're willing to wait.

There is no reason you can't talk about commitment. You must talk. Men tend to be straightforward and action oriented in everything else. Why not this? If you've been dating a man for several months, you have every right to ask, "Do you see this relationship leading to a commitment? Not marriage necessarily, but do you think we would ever get to a point of dating each other exclusively?"

If he runs from this talk of commitment, you've learned something, and you've saved a lot of time. Stop seeing him. (Maybe that will jolt him into making a commitment, but don't count on it.)

If he does talk, you have opened up a valuable line of communication. Now, as your relationship progresses, you can talk honestly about the issues that may hold him back from commitment.

Bash the myths. Together, you need to challenge the Hollywood myths and affirm the truth. Starlets are beautiful, but beauty is not everything. You have much more to offer than just beauty. You are not perfect, but you're good, and good for him. The myths are strong, and they don't die easily, but you are offering him reality.

It is imperative that you set boundaries and observe them. These may be time boundaries. You may need to set a deadline for his decision. You may need to set emotional boundaries. These are less defined, but be careful about giving your heart to him until you know he'll repay you in kind. There are certainly sexual boundaries to observe. It is foolish to give yourself sexually outside of marriage.

Of course you'd expect me, the evangelical Christian counselor, to give you such advice, but I'm not the only one giving it. Increasingly, from secular counselors and authors you hear the same thing. Sex outside a committed relationship is a lie. It gives the impression of intimacy without anything to back it up.

In dealing with a commitment-phobic man, you need to put yourself in a position of strength. If you need him more than he needs you, he will realize that, and he'll take advantage of it. Even if he's a nice guy, he will not commit more than he has to. He sees a commitment as a kind of loss. He needs to see what he'll be gaining. If you are dependent on him and his attention, you are undervaluing yourself.

"Measuring your self-worth by his acceptance or rejection is absurd," write Bonnie Barnes and Tricia Clarke in *How to Get a Man to Make a Commitment.*[4] They propose the Two-Week Program, which is basically refusing to see him and making him think you might be seeing others. It is designed to make him afraid of losing you.

But it's also a way to establish that you have a life of your own. It puts you in a position of strength. Suddenly, you are not begging him to make a commitment but offering him a chance to participate in your amazing life. "Our guidelines emphasize becoming stylish, independent, well-informed, and self-motivated while maintaining a feminine mystique,"

Barnes and Clarke write. "The resulting self-esteem can make a woman so successful and attractive to the opposite sex that she'll never have to use any ploy to manipulate her man into a commitment."[5]

How do you deal with a commitment-phobic man? The answer is not manipulation, but it may involve hard bargaining. If a commitment-phobic man is bent on staying that way, find out and get out—unless you, too, are happy with a casual, noncommitted relationship. If he makes you think that commitment is a possibility, but he never comes through, he's not treating you fairly. You are well within your rights to demand honesty and, within a reasonable time frame, a decision.

Part 3

Changing the System

Chapter Fifteen

Healing the Wounds

In an ancient legend, the Fisher King suffers from a terrible wound. He languishes in his castle, groaning in agony, but still trying to be gracious to all visitors.

I see in this old story a picture of modern man.

In one variation of the legend, visitors are warned not to ask any questions of the Fisher King. And so they don't. They see his pain and long to know how he was wounded. But they do not ask.

Only later do they learn that the question would have cured him. Merely by asking, "Why are you in such pain?" they could have alleviated it.

This, too, is a picture of modern man.

Most men are deeply wounded. But they have built tall castle walls around themselves. When visitors are admitted, they learn not to ask questions. Pain is personal. "I can deal with it."

Yet the right questions, asked in the right way, can help him heal.

The magnitude of the original wound may not be as much of a problem as how deeply it's buried. For some men, the wound might be as seemingly trivial as adorable Suzy saying, "You're ugly!" at age five. If that message got implanted on the consciousness and reaffirmed with every rejection that's occurred over thirty or forty years, that incident can have profound effects.

WHERE DO THE WOUNDS COME FROM?

Let me suggest several possible sources.

Parents

I am regularly overwhelmed by the responsibility of parenting. I do my best to show my children love, but in my darker moments, I fear that I may be doing something wrong that will scar them for life. I guess I have to trust that God will use the best efforts of my wife and myself to create happy children, who grow up to be whole adults.

But I've counseled many adults who are struggling with problems their parents created or passed on. In some cases, the parents were mean to the kids, but most often parents wound their children accidentally. I've talked with people who are hesitant to do the excavation of their past history because they're convinced their parents were wonderful people. They don't want to say anything bad about them. That's understandable. But it's still possible to say, "My parents meant well, but this one thing they did had a negative effect on me, which I'm still dealing with." A man doesn't need to turn parents into ogres, but he does need to unearth the problem that holds him back.

Victimizing Events

Victimizing events might include rape, incest, physical abuse, abandonment, divorce, or a beating by the school bully. These can have profound effects on a male's life long after the events take place.

Often, because of the embarrassment involved, or because of a family's shroud of secrecy, these events are deeply hidden. In some cases, a man blocks them out of his conscious memory. Because of this, the excavation process may require professional counseling.

Losses/Acts of God

The death of a loved one or even a pet can cause great pain in a boy. If he never deals with it properly, it can come out in negative ways later. The grieving process moves through stages and can take quite a while. If it is stunted in some way, the healing never fully happens.

A spiritual question can come up whenever there's an event beyond a child's control: "Why would God let this happen?" It's not easy to answer. But some children conclude that God is against them, that God is a vengeful judge, or that God must not exist. These ideas are then carried into adulthood, and proper spiritual development is hindered.

Failure/Dashed Expectations

I always wanted to be a major league baseball player. Me and a million other kids. But in my early life I *expected* to be a major league baseball player. It was a sobering realization when, sometime in high school, I realized I lacked the skills to do that.

That may seem like a trivial example, but many men have similar stories, which have affected them more deeply. American boys are taught that we can do anything we set our minds to. But when we fall short of our expectations, it's like a punch in the stomach.

For some boys, there's parental pressure to be a doctor or lawyer or athlete or whatever Dad is. When they don't attain that goal, they feel they've disappointed their parents.

There is wholeness in knowing who you are and what you need to do, in learning from your mistakes, in picking yourself up and trying again. But children don't automatically know how to do that. Sometimes a failure or disappointment can leave deep scars.

Authority Figures

Teachers and preachers and coaches can make the same mistakes that parents make. They can wound a child's self-esteem or skew a child's understanding of life. These falsehoods get imprinted on the child's soul.

Classmates

Kids can be cruel to each other. As children try to find their own identity, it's a rough-and-tumble world. Sometimes Billy feels he has to put Johnny down to build himself up.

Such persecution can do great damage, inflicting wounds that often take decades to heal.

Romance

Young love is a pain game. Teenagers make themselves vulnerable as they pledge their undying love to each other. And almost invariably, they break up, causing great grief. Often both parties grieve—one feels the loss, the other the guilt.

I know that both boys and girls engage in teenage romances, and both get hurt. But I believe that boys are especially clueless in the whole business. It's a female thing to major in relationships, and there's a whole female culture that nurtures and nourishes young women in affairs of the heart—moms and sisters and magazines. Guys don't have that. A girl can cry for three days and a colony of friends surrounds her. Guys are expected to stuff the emotion and suit up for the game.

We're still stuffing that emotion.

EXCAVATION

Fran was growing frustrated with Mike's emotional coldness. Before their marriage, he seemed sweet and loving, but now he was a stone wall. After one incident, she angrily yelled, "You have no emotions! What's wrong with you?"

That was a javelin straight at Mike's heart. *She's right*, he thought. *I really don't have feelings. Am I normal?*

That's when they came to me for counseling. I believed that Mike's feelings were probably buried in his past somewhere, so we began our archaeological excavation.

Mike grew up in a military home. His father ran it like a barracks—austere, no emotion shown. There was no hugging. There were no expressions of love. Mike's mother was a mystery to him, extremely passive, almost cowering in the presence of the father. Mike remembers the feeling of calm in the house during the day, when Dad was gone, and how that calm was shattered as he walked in the door.

Mike had no memories before age ten and few before age twelve. He shut off the emotional part of his brain as a coping mechanism. He began to deal logically, factually, with everything. (Remember the ability to compartmentalize?)

He inherited an aggressive and competitive spirit from his father, and he did well at sports in high school and college. In college he met Fran and wooed her with a calculated strategy. He had learned enough from TV and friends to tap into her emotions—but he kept his own hidden away.

As a married man, Mike entered a whole new world. He politely listened to his wife, but he couldn't relate emotionally to her. He didn't know how. He could say the words, but without the feelings.

Fran was baffled until Mike's father came to visit. "I could see a lot of Mike in his father," Fran said, "and I saw why he was the way he was. His father was cold and distant all weekend. I tried to connect with him, to share things about our family, our emotions, the love and concern we felt, but Mike's dad was unable to relate. At one point, while I was talking, he got up and left the room. Then I knew where Mike got it."

With this newfound insight, and through the counseling process, Mike and Fran were able to find some new connections. Fran was patient and gently drew Mike into emotional involvement with her. It will always be a struggle for him, but he is making progress.

In this case, the major source of Mike's wounding was fairly easy to find. You may have to do more digging. And it's possible that your man will not let you near the source of his wounds. They may be too painful, too personal. If so, urge him to see a counselor on his own or together with you. But if your man is willing to work through this with you, you may begin to uncover some of those old problems and begin a healing process.

You must start by establishing a trusting environment. You need to be a cushion for him because he's afraid he'll fall. You cannot badger or judge or hurry him. Nudge gently, and affirm him at each step.

This may require a change of pace for you. Literally. You may need to slow down your pace of expectation and be patient with him as he grasps his memories. Do not put words into his mouth. Do not tell him how he must feel about something. Let him tell you.

Prod him with emotion questions. Do not say, "You must have felt awful about that!" Ask, "How did you feel about that?"

You may push him (gently) for feelings when he gives you thoughts. If he says, "I thought it was strange at the time," you may repeat, "But how did you feel?"

You might give him multiple choice questions, but let him choose the answer: "Did you feel angry, confused, or frustrated?" You might put yourself in his shoes, as long as you withhold judgment: "I think I would have been angry about that. How did you feel?"

At each step, let him know he's okay. He may be afraid that he will hurt you, bore you, or offend you with these memories. Affirm him regularly. Assure him that you do not think any less of him.

If he starts to cry, don't smother. Guys learn that crying is what girls do. So if he starts to cry, do not overly smother him because that would emasculate him. It confirms that you, as a female, are pro-crying, and he, as a hearty male, should be anti-crying. You will want to encourage him because it may signal an emotional breakthrough. But don't draw attention to it by smothering or saying, "There, there. Cry all you want." Get him a tissue, touch him gently, and keep talking.

Be aware of his mixed feelings about people in his past. If, say, a coach abused him, your man may defend this coach: "Don't get the wrong idea. He wasn't a bad guy. He just knocked me senseless one time." Be careful about judging the people he talks about. Focus on the actions rather than the personalities: "Even if he wasn't a bad guy, this coach did a bad thing, right? How did you feel about that?"

Watch out for the old-girlfriend trap. What if it comes out that he's having a hard time loving you because he still mourns the breakup with his high-school sweetheart? How will you feel? If he sees that you are bothered by his revelations, he will feel justified in covering up his feelings again. It's possible that this excavation process will drag you both through the mud. You need to be ready for that.

SETTING THINGS RIGHT

Once you've gone back to the wounding, what do you do then? Your man needs to forgive. Forgiveness is *not* saying that there was no wrong done. Forgiveness does not approve of the transgression. In fact, it comes face-to-face with the misdeed and says, "That was wrong!" But then it's gone. Forgiveness is the decision to be free of the problem. No revenge. I will merely get on with my life.

Your man may need to forgive himself. There may be some past action he feels great shame about. Here again, he may need to ask forgiveness of someone he wronged. But if the person is out of reach, your man should ask God for forgiveness and let the issue rest.

He may need to forgive God. That is, he may be holding a grudge against God for something that God allowed to happen long ago. I've known people who tried to "punish" God by staying away from church or by indulging in some sinful behavior. They're only punishing themselves.

If your man feels this way, I would urge him to have a heart-to-heart talk with God. It's okay to tell God exactly how he feels, even if he has negative feelings. Point him to the example of Jacob, Job, Jeremiah, or the psalmists. God wants to be in a relationship with your man. He wants to set things right.

There is victory in forgiveness. There's a moment when a man says, "I was hurt a long time ago, and I've allowed that hurt to continue for all these years. There's no reason for that. I want to let it go and get on with my life." That's a great moment.

REBUILDING YOUR LIFE

As you seek to work together to build your relationship, after the excavation has been done, you need to keep a couple of points in front of both of you.

That was then; this is now. The ancient wounds belong to the past. New decisions need to be made, based on the present reality.

That was them; this is me. You are not his old girlfriend. You are not his parents. He needs to learn to relate to you as you and to banish the ghosts of his past.

Not long after I was remarried, I got upset with my wife for coming home late from a shopping trip. As I ranted, Lori stopped me and said, "Wait! There's someone else in the room with us."

"Who?" I asked, looking around.

"Your ex-wife."

Sure enough, Lori had done nothing unreasonable. I was just worried because of all the times I had been wounded in the past by lies. I was relating to the ghost of my ex-wife, not to the present wife who had always been truthful.

Pick up where you left off. Your man's emotional growth may have been stunted by the past events you've uncovered. Even after setting things right, he needs to start growing all over again. He may never get to the point where you'd like him to be. But he can make progress. Welcome his progress, each step of the way, but allow for a few stumbles.

Chapter Sixteen

Communication

Men and women speak different languages. Much of the frustration in communication between the sexes results from a language gap.

Therefore, we need a course in intergender communication. We need to teach each other what we mean. In most relationships, since the woman is the gatherer, the guardian of togetherness, she will have to take the lead.

Learning a second language will take a lot of time for your man. Be patient. Don't expect him to change overnight. And he will still probably speak with an accent. You will, too. Your sexual distinctives will not be erased, nor should they be. But at least you and your man should know that two different languages are being spoken and then work at understanding each other.

UNDERSTANDING THE DIFFERENCES

Women use more adjectives and nouns; men use more verbs. And there's a difference in the way men and women put together sentences. Men seem more interested in movement and action while women focus more on psychological states. You probably haven't counted the verbs, but this should not surprise you, considering what we've said about men's action orientation. Sociologist Lucile Duberman notes that these differences show "that men and women have different realities, that they think differently, hold different sets of values, and communicate on different levels."[1]

The early research that Duberman cited has been confirmed by recent studies. Several recent books have raised the issue of communication differences between the sexes. This action language is one key finding.

"For women . . . the key question is 'How *are* you?'" write Naifeh and Smith in *Why Can't Men Open Up?* "For men, it's more likely to be 'How are you doing?' Or 'What have you been up to?'"[2]

Several writers note the male desire to fix things. "In contrast to women's desire for empathy when talking about personal problems, men feel the need to fix things, and do so by offering solutions," writes Michelle Weiner-Davis in *Divorce Busting.*[3]

Consider this scene. A woman comes home from work in tears.

HE: What's the matter?

SHE: My boss is giving me too much work to do. I don't think I can handle anymore.

HE: Did you complain about it?

SHE: Yes, but she just doesn't understand.

HE: Then quit.

SHE: I can't do that.

HE: Why not? If they're not going to appreciate you, just leave. You can find something else.

SHE: It's not that bad.

HE: Well, if you're going to come home in tears, it *is* that bad. You shouldn't let them treat you like that.

They are talking right past each other. When she comes home in tears, she is sharing. He thinks she is begging for help. She wants him to hold her and feel her feelings with her. He thinks she wants him to figure out how to solve her problem.

When she rejects his solution, he responds by putting her down. It's a logical point: Either her emotions are out of control, or she is too cowardly to change her situation. Either way, she loses.

Deborah Tannen says that in conversation, men convey information while women express emotion. Men use "report talk" while women use "rapport talk." Thus, men can preserve a certain emotional independence and stay somewhat above the conversation. Women use conversation to "maintain intimacy and create connections."

An article in the June 22, 1993, issue of *USA Today* summed up some key points of Tannen's *You Just Don't Understand:* "The differences cause her to see him as self-centered and domineering. He sees her as a babblemouth, illogical and insecure."

TRANSLATING

Men have well-developed systems of communication, which they use in various areas of life. Author Roy McCloughry puts his finger on the problem, observing that

> the concepts of extreme rationality, problem-solving and "report talk" which have served men well in public life do

> not work well in personal relationships. Not showing weakness, regarding others as competitors and being ambitious are not helpful in a relationship where intimacy and disclosure are expected.
>
> The fact is that many men are inarticulate emotionally. One of the most striking things about the outpouring of women's writing has been their ability to express even the most delicate nuances of emotion deep inside them. Many men have no personal language with which to describe the inner emotional world.[4]

But I believe that intergender communication is possible. A man can learn to use emotional language, though he may never be fluent in it. And you can learn to communicate well with your man. It involves understanding his language, conversing (sometimes) in his language, and helping him to understand yours.

1. BODY LANGUAGE

Men are often more physical than verbal. They may not know how to express words of love, but they will hug and kiss and so on. And they may not always express negative emotions, such as grief or anger, but they may show women physically how they feel.

Learn to Read Your Man's Body Language

Is he open or closed? Is he smiling or scowling? Is he relaxed or tense? Is he turned toward you or turned away? You don't need a degree to interpret these basic signals. Other signals will be unique to your man. You need to learn what he means by them.

Draw His Body Language Out into Words

Ask him how he feels. If his body is in a closed stance, stop and ask, "Are you really interested in this?" Maybe he's trying to tell you it would be better to talk another time. As always, use questions or "I statements" rather than "you statements." Don't assume that you're reading him correctly. To the man who's being read, body language interpretation can be maddening when it's wrong and scary when it's right. Ask him whether you're reading him right and whether he'd like to talk about it.

Use Touch to Communicate

One woman noted, "When [my husband] and I are having a fight or disagreement, and things are going downhill fast, I'll just reach over and touch him. The whole conversation changes. We'll still talk about it, we'll still have a disagreement, but we won't be as angry with each other."[5]

You can also teach your man to use touch to communicate with you. Tell him what casual touches can mean to you. While men are often highly physical in sports and sex, they're not always gentle. You can introduce your man to a whole new vocabulary of gentle, loving touch. Tell him what you like and what it means to you.

Watch Your Body Language

You may say, "Talk to me," but if your body language is closed or reflects annoyance, he may interpret this as "talk to me so I can tell you how wrong you are." You don't mean to communicate this, but if that's what he reads, he will shut down emotionally, turning off the conversation.

2. ACTIVE LISTENING

Active listening is a matter of paying attention in a conversation, supporting the other person, and interacting freely.

Take a look at your listening habits and see whether you could do some work to draw out the man in your life. Put yourself in his place. Imagine his feelings, and get him to talk on that level: "What did you think about that? How did you feel?" Be interested in what's inside your man, and let your questions flow.

The best way to draw out a man who has difficulty sharing his emotions is to listen to him. He may not talk as often as you'd like, so you want to make sure that when he does talk, you encourage more of the same. Here are some suggested rules for active listening:

- Watch your body language. Be open, accepting.
- Don't interrupt—even if you have something brilliant to say.
- Don't personalize. Don't assume that everything he says is about you. Don't assume that if he's unhappy, you have to make him happy.
- Watch your reactions. Don't overreact to what he says.
- Don't give advice or try to solve the problem.
- Don't steal the attention. You say, "Oh, yes, I had an experience like that!" Sounds like you're getting involved, but you're stealing the focus. If you do this, quickly turn it back toward him.
- Ignore or remove distractions.
- Mirror. This is sometimes known as reflective listening. Clarify your man's statements by repeating what he has said, but always throw the focus back to him.

3. OPEN-ENDED QUESTIONS

Contrast these two conversations.

SHE: Hi, hon, did you have good day?
HE: Uh-huh.

SHE: Are you hungry?
HE: Uh-huh.
SHE: You look tired, did you have a rough day?
HE: Uh-huh.
SHE: What's the matter? Did the boss get to you again?
HE: Uh-huh.
SHE: Still working on that same project?
HE: Uh-huh.

SHE: Hi, hon, what was your day like?
HE: Well, let me think. . . . It was actually kind of rough. . . . It started with my boss coming into my office and . . .

The conversation goes on from there. At first, the husband may not know what to talk about, but if you listen actively and are patient, he may get into it. He gets to talk about what he wants to talk about. He sets the direction and the outcome for the conversation. And he does the work while you listen, reflect, and empathize. This question may be followed with some mirroring about his day or his feelings or with another open-ended question: "What do you feel like doing tonight?"

Open-ended questions might not always open up a man, but they are your best shot. With practice and patience, he might even get used to talking to you and enjoying the conversation. The ultimate improvement would be to have him adapt this skill and begin to say to you, "Well, enough about me, dear. How was your day?"

"Inexpressive males are often struggling within themselves for words that describe their feelings, thoughts, or reactions," writes James E. Kilgore. "Frequently they lose the battle and remain silent. Sometimes the woman relating to an inexpressive male has to develop patience in order not to put her words in his mouth."[6]

So you need to avoid rhetorical or loaded questions ("You're going to wear that?"). Stay away from value-loaded questions as well ("Why don't you ever take me out to dinner?"). Let your body language and tone of voice cooperate with your overall purpose—encouraging your man to express himself.

4. EMOTIONAL WORD PICTURES

I've already mentioned men's difficulty in expressing their emotions. Sometimes it helps to draw a picture or at least a word picture.[7]

When children are learning to read, they use books with lots of pictures. Even the language in the books is picturesque. It helps to see something, in your mind's eye, if you're trying to understand it. When Jesus taught the great truths of God's kingdom, He used word pictures—we call them parables—simple stories that expressed deep truths.

Sometimes word pictures can help us "get" things that we wouldn't otherwise understand or want to understand.

In my family we have often used word pictures to describe hard-to-grasp feelings. We've made a game out of it. I know it helps me to tap into the right side, the creative side, of my brain.

When I'm clicking off emotionally, my wife will take the time to think up a story to tell me how she feels. I might stonewall a more direct approach, but she gets me through the story.

As you develop word pictures to communicate with your man, try to delve into his world for your examples—his job, his sports teams, his hobbies, and so on. Soon you should get the hang of it. It may be even harder for your man if he is not as right-brained as you are. But keep at it. (It's also a good way to communicate with kids.)

SOLVING PROBLEMS

Remember that feelings are a foreign language for many men. You may have to tell your man what you need from him. He will try to fix your feelings. Tell him that you need a hug. He will want to know whether he's successful in comforting you. Give him a progress report. You don't have to pretend to feel better if you don't (or if you don't want to), but talk openly with him about what you need from him.

Get used to using the words *I feel.* Don't say, "What you're doing is so inconsiderate!" Say, "I feel neglected when you do that. I feel that you don't care for me."

You and your man need to arrive at a shared reality. You are used to thinking that what you feel is real. He thinks that what he perceives is real. So if you jump on him for being inconsiderate, you think it's real because you feel it, but he didn't intend to be inconsiderate, so he thinks you're imagining things. You disagree on what's real in this situation.

But he has to agree that he did the particular thing that bothered you. And he has to agree that it bothers you. Your feelings are real, whether their cause is real or imagined. So you can reach a point of shared reality by saying, "When you do this, it makes me feel this way." You're not saying it's right or wrong—you're merely saying that it *is*. He can affect how you feel by his behavior. If he wants you not to feel bad, he won't do the thing that offends you.

This is male talk—objective, extremely rational, action oriented. You are translating your feelings into his language.

Don't use words like *never* and *always*. You may feel this way, but these words are usually not precisely accurate—and that can give your man a loophole. If you are complaining about something he *almost* never does, be precise about how often.

Try the sandwich technique. Sandwich a negative between two positives. Do this not for manipulative purposes but for loving purposes. Your goal is to have the message heard, and the best way to have it heard by a defensive man is to say it as lovingly as possible: "I really care about you, but it hurt me when you said that today. I know you didn't mean to hurt my feelings." There's a sandwich he should be able to stomach.

If you are having an ongoing problem with your man, see if you can agree on what the problem is. It's amazing to me how often couples can't agree on what they're fighting over. Use active listening, open-ended questions, and word pictures to discuss what's at issue. Avoid one-sided descriptions of the problem: "Our problem is that you're too lazy." Try a balanced approach: "I have lots of energy, and when you come home from work, you're tired."

Set Goals for Your Relationship

Your man may respond to a challenge like this. If you agree that your marriage is a 4 on a scale of 10, maybe you can discuss specific ways to move it toward a 10. You may engage his competitive, action-oriented spirit. Men run scared from the vague "Let's talk about our relationship." But a more specific "How can we improve our relationship?" might be more appealing.

Try to Identify One or Two Issues to Work On

Men get overwhelmed by large lists, but if you can go from a 4 to a 5 by working on one issue, your man may climb on board. Remember that men generally need to be told what to do. So be as specific and measurable as possible in setting your goals.

I've encouraged women to set goals as specific as this: "I want a half hour of conversation with my husband each day. I want three back rubs from my husband each week." If a man knows that a simple task can improve his marriage, he may be motivated to do it.

Celebrate Success

If you've gone from a 4 to a 5, stop and party a little before you move on to a 6. A man needs affirmation, and he'll get overwhelmed if you move on to the next task too soon.

Mind Your Timing

Choose the right time to work with your husband on difficult issues. Late at night is probably not the best time if he'll be tired then. You may also need to give him fair warning so that he can plan his approach to a relationship talk: "We really need to work on some things, honey. How about this Sunday after brunch? Would that be okay?" If a more immediate problem surfaces late at night, don't be afraid to sleep on it. In general I agree that you should not go to bed angry, but it may help if you can call a truce overnight, to start fresh in the light of day.

Pick Your Battles

You will not change every disagreeable thing about your man. Don't get overwhelmed by the myriad issues in your relationship. Choose the most important one, and stay focused on that.

A biblical phrase has guided me through many communication issues: "speaking the truth in love" (Eph. 4:15). We need to confront sometimes, to speak the truth even when it's difficult to do so. We need to hold others accountable for their actions. But we must always communicate in love.

Chapter Seventeen

It Takes Two

In the counseling field we study family systems. The systems approach understands that any change in one family member will affect all other members. If you're married to a man who seems to love you too little, you must also look to yourself and your ways of interacting to bring about change to the system.

In her book *Divorce Busting*, Michelle Weiner-Davis illustrates this point by what she calls the butterfly effect:

> Noted meteorologist Edward Lorenz was attempting to analyze the effects a small change would have on global weather patterns. He discovered that even the most minute changes have profound effects on complex systems like weather. Lorenz described the dynamic of nearly imperceptible changes resulting in enormous changes—as he put it, a butterfly flapping its wings in Brazil might create a tornado in Texas.[1]

Minute, but significant, changes in you can create ripple effects that may completely change your marriage within time. I prefer to have both members of the marriage in the session because then change can occur in tandem and be understood by both parties. But whenever I have one to work with, I'll take what I can get. As you get healthier, the system will change.

Let me offer a few cautions, however. First, I do not mean to imply that you are to blame for the problems in your marriage. If your man is loving too little and showing it in any of the ways I've described here, he must bear responsibility for that. I don't blame you for causing his behavior or for allowing his behavior to occur, and you shouldn't blame yourself. All I'm saying is that some adjustments on your part may change the balance in your relationship.

Second, maybe your attempts to change the system will yield little or no response from your man. But it's worth a try. And at least you will have changed yourself in some positive way.

Finally, there are times when one spouse is getting healthier and that affects the relationship negatively:

- An abused wife begins to speak up and set boundaries, which increases the husband's anger.
- The alcoholic stops drinking, which allows him or her to start feeling the pain of an unfulfilling marriage.
- The wife confronts her husband about his infidelity, and that causes the husband to file for divorce.

These examples of seemingly negative effects can occur when one person in the relationship changes for the better. But don't let that keep you from making healthy changes. It's worth the risk. Your changes may throw your system into turmoil for a while, but eventually, it may settle down to a more balanced relationship.

THE SYSTEMS APPROACH

It takes two to tango. Even though one partner may be doing all the work, it still takes two to form a relationship. Again and again, I find that men who love too little are in relationships with women who exhibit certain tendencies. Which came first, the men's lack of love or the women's enabling tendencies? I don't know. Probably the two developed together, interweaving into what is now a tapestry of frustration. But perhaps, by pulling one thread, we can unravel that. Let's look at some examples.

The Clinger and the Backer

Some women are overly dependent. They need their men to be with them frequently, and they require a lot of emotional reinforcement. They always seem to be digging for the inner feelings of their men. Such women cling tightly to their men.

Clinging women violate boundaries. I think of a "Seinfeld" episode involving the close talker, a man who would talk to people face-to-face, almost literally nose-to-nose, invading their personal space. A clinging woman can invade a man's emotional space.

The natural response to a close talker is to back away. And emotionally, men who are in relationships with clinging women often back away. They withdraw emotionally, which is exactly what their women *don't* want. It's a matter of self-preservation. They need to reclaim their emotional selves before their women steal all their feelings. They become passive, shutting down because they are overwhelmed by the intensity of their women's emotional dependency.

Men can become controlling in such situations if they see their women's dependency as a means of power for themselves. They can dole out occasional rewards of emotional affirmation but generally ignore or even abuse their women.

In *Love Must Be Tough*, James Dobson discusses the problem of husbands feeling "trapped in suffocating relationships with women they clearly disrespect." He advises women to open the trap and let their partners out. He's not recommending divorce but the end of "techniques of containment," which include "manipulative grief, anger, guilt and appeasement. Begging, pleading, crying, hand-wringing and playing the role of the doormat are equally destructive."[2]

"By being independent and giving instead of dependent and demanding, a woman can subdue the fear of dependency that keeps a man at arm's length emotionally," write Naifeh and Smith in *Why Can't Men Open Up?*

> She can be the one to whom he comes for respite from the demands of masculinity and independence. . . . By being dependent and needy, a woman invites a man to withdraw emotionally. The moment she becomes independent, elusive, and mysterious, a man will climb mountains to go after her.[3]

The Nag and the Caveman

The woman who nags the man in her life can be emotionally dependent, but she tends to be more controlling. Do this; do that. I need this; I need that. In response, a man will often retreat to his cave. He will seek some solitude, a respite from his woman's onslaught. Yet she often stands at the mouth of the cave, continuing to nag.

A home with this system will be a volatile one, with many arguments, yet it may be healthier than the home where the disagreements are hidden.

This brings to mind a question: Which came first? Does she nag because he's so passive, or did he shut down because of her nagging? Probably both. It probably started small at first, and it has continued in a downward spiral. Or, if you will, a dance.

The Perfectionist and the Underachiever

The perfectionist finds fault with everything her man does. She lives by a certain standard and expects everyone else to live by that standard.

Perfectionists often have major self-esteem issues. Sometimes they are proud and consider everyone else inferior. But more often perfectionists (especially women) measure themselves by the same impossibly high standards and come up short. Such a woman is very hard on herself, second-guessing her actions and plaguing herself with guilt. Of course, perfectionists of both types tend to criticize the work of others—especially the men in their lives.

Perfectionistic women are always trying to fine-tune their men. Even if their men are pretty good to them, they see what their men are *not* doing or what they're doing wrong rather than what they're doing right.

This reaction can lead a man into passive-aggression and underachievement. A man gets discouraged when the things he does for the woman he loves are never good enough. At first he may strive to please her, but soon he realizes that he will never please her, so what's the use of trying? A man can give up. He may continue to attempt things for the woman, but he won't give that extra effort. He'll learn to put up with the woman's criticism. The system gets firmly entrenched. He gives a less-than-full effort, and she scolds him for it, which prompts him to keep underachieving.

With the woman being so assertive, the man can learn that the best response is compliance. He will quietly pretend to try to please her, but he may seek to get even in other areas. He may express his passive-aggression by sabotaging his work for her or he may stop talking with her, criticize her in the presence of others, or spend more and more hours at work. Passive-aggressive men in relationships with perfectionistic women are especially prone to infidelity. And they're looking not for sexual thrills but for admiration. They need to feel significant, and so they may find that significance in other relationships.

The solution for a couple in the perfectionistic system must be to redefine what is good enough. The woman must ease her standards. This is extremely difficult, but a relationship may be at stake. She must start within herself. She may need to start with professional help to shore up her self-esteem.

Then she must monitor the demands she makes on her man. I would suggest listing all demands made in a week. Then cut the list in half—the next week, try to demand less. She must learn to affirm the man verbally for good things that he does. In addition, she must learn to appreciate progress and effort, not just a perfect finished project.

She should give her man permission to respond honestly to her demands. She should seek his opinion rather than pronounce judgment on everything. And she should ask how he feels about certain tasks.

All of this requires breaking a standard, and it can be painful. "With perfectionism, the baseline issue is control," says my colleague Melanie van Pletsen.

> So you have to learn to be comfortable with being out of control. You life's not going to feel right until you achieve that. You may need to "fake it till you make it," but that is your goal, to not give into the compulsion to fix it, to take charge, to do it right, to criticize.[4]

Meanwhile, the man must reengage with her, invest himself once again in the relationship, stop pretending, and say what he honestly feels: "No, it's not a professional job, but it's a good amateur job, and it's all we can afford right now, okay?"

The Victim and the Savior/Abuser

Many women seem to go through life as victims. They tend to have a lot of baggage from the past, deep wounds from previous victimization, a lot of unresolved conflicts. They get into difficult relationships, often with unavailable men or even abusive men.

Some psychologists have suggested that women seek men who are like their fathers, and they try to change them into what they wanted their fathers to be. So if a father is emotionally distant, unavailable, or self-centered, the daughter will grow up to seek emotionally distant, unavailable, or self-centered men. She will try to win the attention from her boyfriend or husband that she could never win from her father.

Judith Sills suggests that some people, especially people who have grown up in abusive homes, have a need to create drama. They grew up with chaos, passion, violence—and that's how they think life needs to be. "If life becomes too stable, too mundane, too predictable to stir much feeling," Sills writes to such a person, "you will create the stimulation, staging dramatic family battles, choosing impossible partners, risking your job, flouting the social rules, just to get a rise out of yourself."[5]

Those who have been genuinely victimized, especially in childhood, have had their personal boundaries crossed and damaged. So now they have no boundaries. They allow people to enter their lives and take advantage of them because they never learned when or how to say no. I see this often in the case of women who were sexually abused as children. Now they regularly find themselves in the role of sexual victim, and they wonder why. I suspect they don't put up sexual boundaries, and men take advantage of their defenseless position.

Men tend to take one of two roles in response to the victim. Some men have a Messiah complex. They see a woman who has been victimized, and they want to "save" her. They pamper and coddle and affirm her. If these saviors succeed in nursing her back to health, they often find that she's not interested in them anymore. There's not enough drama. Health is boring. So these men learn that they have a vested interest in keeping the woman in the role of victim, and even the kindest savior type becomes a controlling man.

Many other men, however, will take advantage of the victim. These are self-absorbed men, who need an encourager, a secretary, or a lover; or these are controlling men, who get their kicks from running someone else's life. Often these are abusers, who physically and emotionally add to the woman's victimization.

And so a man and a woman may be in a system of violence and control. It may be something they feel comfortable with, even though it's damaging both of them. Perhaps they don't know any other way to relate.

She may feel no power or responsibility to change the situation.

I would seek to empower the victim to take responsibility for her life. She needs to make her own choices. She needs to stand up to the abuse or remove herself from it.

The controlling man needs to see the victimized woman as a person of value, as a person who can make choices for herself. If there is abuse going on, it has to stop. Hard-core abusers are hard to stop. They will probably seek to revictimize the woman or find another victim. But men with less serious problems can improve their behavior by seeing their own value, apart from the issue of whom they control, and seeing the value of their partner.

SOME STRATEGIES FOR CHANGE

These are just a few of the more common systems I have found with men who love too little and the women who love them. You may have an entirely different system or a variation of one of them. In discussing each of these four systems, I suggested certain methods of change, but let me add some general strategies.

Trace Your Dance

Who taught you to dance? Of course, I'm talking about the unhealthy-system dance. Where did you learn it? From your parents? From friends? Are you self-taught? Or is it totally a response to your man's off-center behavior? You may need to do some excavation on your own to uncover old wounds and start the healing process.

Do You Love Too Little?

Sometimes women are afraid of true intimacy. And that's why they fall for men who love too little. There's a certain comfort in knowing that he won't get too close—and you can blame him for that distance. You're off the hook. You can still play the role of guardian of the relationship, and your emotional walls will never be crossed.

If you're like this, you need to ask yourself, "What do I really want?" Some women are torn—wanting intimacy but afraid of it. They give mixed signals to their men: "I want you, I want you, but please stay away." The best remedy is to talk about it.

Accept the Vulnerability of Conversation

Talk about where you are and what you're doing. As you try to change the system, it shouldn't be a secret. Say, "I'm trying to be stronger and less dependent. I'd like your help."

If you're trying to curb your perfectionism, you can say, "I'm fighting the urge to criticize your work, dear. I can find something wrong with it—I *always* find something wrong—but I do appreciate your help." Such honesty makes you vulnerable, but it's the best way to create lasting change.

Make Creative Use of Games and Rituals

Systems don't change naturally. You have to create new systems. One way to do that is to establish new games or rituals. I mean, start the Friday Night Fights. (You will need a good sense of humor to pull this off. If you and your partner can't laugh at yourselves, it will never work.) If you have a passive-aggressive man, this can draw him out. Start a tradition of having an open, honest fight each Friday night. You tell me what's bothering you. I'll tell you what I don't like. We'll fight fair. We'll listen. Maybe we'll even have a pillow fight to let out our tensions. Then we'll go out for ice cream.

Or on the fifteenth of each month, write a letter to each other in which you talk about the relationship, good and bad.

Have an annual Role Reversal Saturday. For a whole day, imitate each other. That might help you see things from the other's perspective.

Surely you can come up with other ideas that will deal with your unique problems. The point is that games and rituals are intentional, mutually decided system breakers. You agree to do something different—even if it seems silly. And some of these ideas are silly. They're supposed to be. But they may break you out of a rut.

OPPOSITION FROM SURPRISING SOURCES

Changing the system is challenging. Both you and your man have learned to live in certain ways. You have certain ruts of interaction, and it's hard to climb out of them. Even if you succeed in changing your behavior, your man will probably resist. He is used to the system as it is now. He may try to goad you into returning to your nagging or clinging ways. It may take a while for him to trust that you have changed, and even longer for him to change his ways—if he changes at all.

But there may also be outside pressure to stay in your unhealthy system. Your parents may not understand the changes you're trying to make. If you have children, they may resist change. Your community of friends and acquaintances may reinforce the old system and discourage you from changing it. I hope your church supports and strengthens you. I hope you find courage there that helps you decide to change your system from bad to good. Unfortunately, some churches don't encourage such change.

A SUCCESS STORY

Peggy came to me for counseling, frustrated with her passive-aggressive husband, Len. Ideally, I'd like to be meeting with both partners, but Peggy explained that Len didn't believe in psychology. So Peggy had to go it alone, trying to change this relationship unilaterally.

"He excludes me at every turn," she complained.

She looked down, almost guiltily: "I'm suspicious now, so I've been probing more and more. And I've caught him in some lies and half-truths. Those business meetings have sometimes been meetings with his buddies at the local bar. Fortunately, I don't think he's having an affair or anything—I almost wish that *was* the problem. The simple truth is, he doesn't want to be with me."

To my surprise, Peggy followed all my suggestions. For several weeks, she disengaged from him. She was pleasant, not angry, letting him go anywhere he pleased with no nagging, no questions. In fact, when Len announced that he was going out, she'd say something like, "Oh, that sounds good. I think I'll go out with Barb."

This response confused him.

A few months later, Len was going on a short business trip, and Peggy really wanted to go along. Would she sink back into her old nagging techniques? I advised her to ask—without pleading—if she could go along. If he resisted, she should back off, saying, "That's fine. I'd love to come, but it's your choice." Those words seemed strange to her, so she practiced saying them.

And that's what happened. She asked to go. He said, "You wouldn't like it. You'll be bored." And she gave the reply she had practiced.

He went off on his trip alone, but when he returned, he brought her flowers.

A few weeks later, on a Monday, Len announced that he had a dinner to attend with some business associates on Friday.

"Oh," Peggy said calmly. "Will the others be bringing their wives?"

"Some of them," said Len. "But you wouldn't want to go. Sometimes we go pretty late."

"That's okay."

"It's really boring," Len added. "You wouldn't have any fun."

"Okay," said Peggy, disengaging once again. "If you don't want me there, that's fine. I'd really like to go, but it's your choice."

That night, in bed, they talked. They talked about their feelings. He was still afraid of her anger; he didn't believe her change was real. She assured him that she was different; she was playing by new rules. She would not be hanging on him emotionally. She had to establish her sense of self.

He truly seemed to understand.

The next day, he invited her to the dinner on Friday.

Peggy came into my office for her next session, beaming. She explained the most recent developments and said, "We've changed the system. It's all different now. We're doing a lot better."

"One other thing," she added. "Len would like you to recommend a counselor that he could see. Any ideas?"

Notes

Chapter 1

1. A. J. Rudy and R. Peller, *Medical Aspects of Sexuality*, September 1972, pp. 84–86.
2. Steven Naifeh and Gregory White Smith, *Why Can't Men Open Up?*, (New York: Warner, 1984), pp. 4–5.
3. Adapted from Joe Tannenbaum's *Male and Female Realities* (Sugarland, Tex.: Candle Pub. Co., 1989), p. 45.
4. Bob Hicks, *Uneasy Manhood* (Nashville: Thomas Nelson, 1991), p. 31.
5. Anne Moir and David Jessel, *Brain Sex* (New York: Dell, 1989), pp.5–8.
6. Adapted from Moir and Jessel's *Brain Sex*, p. 40.

Chapter 2

1. Moir and Jessel, *Brain Sex*, pp. 20–25.
2. Tannenbaum, *Male and Female Realities*, p. 53.

Chapter 3

1. Tannenbaum, *Male and Female Realities*, pp. 35–45.
2. John Gray, *Men Are from Mars, Women Are from Venus* (New York: HarperCollins, 1992), pp. 31–33.

Chapter 5

1. Deborah Tannen, *You Just Don't Understand* (New York: Simon and Schuster, 1991).
2. Robert Hicks, *The Masculine Journey* (Colorado Springs: NavPress, 1993), p. 78.
3. Patrick Arnold, *Wildmen, Warriors and Kings* (New York: Crossroad, 1991), p. 101, cited by Hicks, *Masculine Journey*, p. 75.
4. Robert Bly, *Iron John* (Reading, Mass.: Addison-Wesley, 1990), p. 146, cited by Hicks, *Masculine Journey*, p. 75.
5. Gray, *Men Are from Mars*, pp. 177ff.

Chapter 6

1. John Updike, "The Disposable Rocket," *Michigan Quarterly Review*, cited in *Harper's*, November 1993, p. 17.

Chapter 7

1. Warren T. Farrell cited in Lucile Duberman, "Beyond Masculinity: Liberating Men and Their Relationships with Women," in *Gender and Sex in Society* (New York: Praeger, 1975), p. 224.
2. Judith Segal, *Dealing with Difficult Men* (Chicago: Contemporary Books, 1993).

Chapter 8

1. Warren T. Farrell cited in Duberman's "Beyond Masculinity," pp. 225–26.
2. Jack Balswick, *Why I Can't Say I Love You* (Waco, Tex.: Word, 1978), cited by James E. Kilgore, *The Intimate Man* (Nashville: Abingdon, 1984), p. 55.
3. Kilgore, *The Intimate Man*, p. 56.
4. Gray, *Men Are from Mars*, p. 31.

Chapter 9

1. *USA Today*, June 22, 1993.
2. Moir and Jessel, *Brain Sex*, p. 19.
3. Moir and Jessel, *Brain Sex*, p. 80.
4. Tannenbaum, *Male and Female Realities*, pp. 77–91.
5. Segal, *Dealing with Difficult* Men, pp. 14–16.
6. Tannenbaum, *Male and Female Realities*, p. 127.

Chapter 11

1. Gray, *Men Are from Mars*, p. 133.
2. Gray, *Men Are from Mars*, p. 76.

Chapter 12

1. Scott Wetzler, *Living with the Passive-Aggressive Man* (New York: Simon and Schuster, 1992).
2. Wetzler, *Living with the Passive-Aggressive Man*, pp. 121–123.

Chapter 13

1. Vincent Gallagher, *Three Compulsions that Defeat Most Men* (Minneapolis: Bethany House, 1992), p. 88.
2. Gerald G. May, *Addiction and Grace* (San Francisco: Harper and Row, 1988), p. 45.

Chapter 14

1. Segal, *Dealing with Difficult Men*, pp. 54–55.
2. American Psychiatric Association, *Diagnostic and Statistical Manual of Mental Disorders*, rev. 3rd ed. (Washington, D.C.: American Psychiatric Association, 1987), p. 351.
3. American Psychiatric Association, *Diagnostic and Statistical Manual*, p. 350.
4. Bonnie Barnes and Tricia Clarke, *How to Get a Man to Make a Commitment* (New York: St. Martin's, 1985), p. 146.
5. Barnes and Clarke, *How to Get a Man to Make a Commitment*, p. 149.

Chapter 16

1. Duberman, *Gender and Sex in Society*, p. 72. Duberman cites sociological research by Diana W. Washay and Nancy Barron.
2. Naifeh and Smith, *Why Can't Men Open Up?*, p. 116.
3. Michelle Weiner-Davis, *Divorce Busting* (New York: Simon and Schuster, 1992), p. 49.
4. Roy McCloughry, "The Yoke of Masculinity," *On Being*, August 1993, p. 16. *On Being* is an Australian Christian magazine. McCloughry is author of *Men and Masculinity* (London: Hodder and Stoughton, 1993).
5. Naifeh and Smith, *Why Can't Men Open Up?*, p. 124.
6. Kilgore, *The Intimate Man*, p. 32.
7. This idea is developed by John Trent and Gary Smalley, *The Language of Love* (Pomona, Calif.: Focus on the Family, 1988).

Chapter 17

1. Weiner-Davis, *Divorce Busting*, p. 92.
2. James Dobson, *Love Must Be Tough* (Dallas: Word, 1993), p. 45.

3. Naifeh and Smith, *Why Can't Men Open Up?*, p. 96.
4. Melanie Van Pletsen, conversation with author, May 11, 1994.
5. Judith Sills, *Excess Baggage* (New York: Penguin, 1993), p. 185.

About the Authors

Thomas Whiteman, Ph.D., is a licensed psychologist who speaks on relational issues around the country. He is the founder of Fresh Start™ Seminars, a divorce recovery program for adults and children. Whiteman is the author of several books on relationships, including *Becoming Your Own Best Friend*, *Flying Solo*, *Love Gone Wrong*, and *The Fresh Start™ Single Parenting Workbook*. He currently lives in Berwyn, Pennsylvania.

Randy Petersen is a freelance writer who has collaborated with Thomas Whiteman on several projects, including *Becoming Your Own Best Friend* and *Love Gone Wrong*. He is a former editor of the *Evangelical Newsletter* and has been active as a leader in several church-related activities. He currently lives in Paoli, Pennsylvania.